FOREST NEIGHBORS

Books by
Edith M. Patch

FOREST NEIGHBORS

by

Edith M. Patch
and
Carroll Lane Fenton

drawings by

Carroll Lane Fenton

YESTERDAY'S CLASSICS

ITHACA, NEW YORK

This edition, first published in 2022 by Yesterday's Classics, an imprint of Yesterday's Classics, LLC, is an unabridged republication of the text originally published by The Macmillan Company in 1938. For the complete listing of the books that are published by Yesterday's Classics, please visit www.yesterdaysclassics.com. Yesterday's Classics is the publishing arm of Gateway to the Classics which presents the complete text of hundreds of classic books for children at www.gatewaytotheclassics.com.

ISBN: 978-1-63334-065-7

Yesterday's Classics, LLC
PO Box 339
Ithaca, NY 14851

TO

ERNEST THOMPSON SETON

whose books on woodcraft have helped many young
naturalists, and whose volumes on *Lives of Game
Animals* contain very much of interest to those
who wish to know more about the
four-footed neighbors of the
North Woods

CONTENTS

FOREST NEIGHBORS

Pines and moosewoods grow together in this part of the forest.

CHAPTER I

THE NORTH WOODS

WOULD you like to follow the tracks of deer and meet their neighbors? Would you like to find the big antlers that a moose has shed? Would you like to eat some spicy checkerberries? Would you like to hear a loon "laugh" early in the morning, and at dusk hear a fox bark or a great horned owl sound his hunting call?

You may have those interesting adventures, and many others, in a forest. A forest, a dictionary will tell you, is a "woodland—a large tract of land covered with trees." But the dictionary will not tell you what a very good time you and your comrades can have there. It will not say a word about the woodland hikes, nor mention the games that give you as much fun as the chipmunks have, when they chase one another round and round the roots of trees.

Where can you find a place like that to visit? If you travel north, south, east, and west, you will find that forests cover many parts of North America. There are dense growths of great trees in Alaska and on the hot sandy lowlands of Florida. Parts of what is called the "Central Hardwood Forest Region" may be found from

1

southern Michigan to northern Alabama. You may visit many woodlands in the Atlantic States or go into the Pacific Coast Forest Region where there are more than sixty million acres of forest land. And even if you travel to all these places, there will still be some of the North American forests that you do not see. For example, there will still be the Rocky Mountain Forests. And there will still be the trees growing from northern Maine to northern Minnesota, and from New Brunswick to Manitoba—forests that we may call the "North Woods."

Before we began to write *Forest Neighbors,* we had to choose one of these many regions, for of course we could not include two of them in one small book. We might have chosen the Rocky Mountain Forests if we had not already told you about some of the trees and animals there in *Mountain Neighbors.* Indeed, any of these regions would have been interesting but we hope you will be glad that we decided to devote this book to the "North Woods."

If you visit a forest, you will see that not all the land is covered with trees. You will find water there, for a forest could not exist without it. That is why some of the forest neighbors are creatures who live in lakes or streams or swamps.

So, if you come to the North Woods, you need not be surprised to find loons there as much at home in Walloon's lake as deer are in woodland trails. And beavers busy themselves in Poplar Creek as naturally as chickadees and many other birds fly among the trees.

Though all the neighbors mentioned in this book

dwell in the North Woods, creatures like most of them live in other forests, too. Mah-kay's cubs picked berries in western Ontario. But other black-bear cubs like hers, or nearly like hers, go berrying in Alaska, in Maine, in New York, in Georgia, in California, and in many other places.

You cannot meet the particular Wah-boos mentioned in this book anywhere except near his home in the North Woods, for he does not travel far. But varying hares, or snowshoe "rabbits," of the same kind (or species) leave their tracks on snowy slopes from Maine to the Rocky Mountains.

Tree frogs like Hyla Versi-color live in different parts of North America from southern Canada to some places in the Gulf States. So perhaps you yourself have heard music just like his trills. Or perhaps you have heard the different tunes of "Cricket Frogs" or "Whistling Frogs" or "Little Chorus Frogs" or "Cowbell Frogs" or "Spring-peepers" or some of the very many other tree frogs that sing in the spring, here and there. For whether you live in the southeastern State of Florida or the northwestern State of Washington, you have some interesting tree frogs for neighbors.

While you are waiting to meet some of the birds and furry animals in the forest, there are many things to interest you. For example, you may learn which of the trees and other plants you see are evergreens. An "evergreen" is a plant that has green leaves all the year round. It sheds its leaves when they are ready to drop, but it does not shed them all at one time. It waits until

The white pine is an evergreen and a conifer.

new leaves come before it drops the old ones. So it is green in spring, summer, autumn, and winter.

In the North Woods, you will find partridge berries and some other low-growing evergreen plants that are covered by snow in the winter. As for the trees, all the cone-bearing trees (conifers) in these woods are evergreen, except the tamarack. The tamarack (also called "larch" and "hackmatack") belongs to the Pine Family, as do all the other conifers. But unlike its relatives, the tamarack sheds all its leaves every fall. After its clusters of narrow leaves turn yellow and drop during the autumn days, its branches remain bare until spring.

White cedars grow in a low, moist part of the forest.

As you walk through the woods, you will notice that the leaves of most of the conifers are narrow— they are awl-shaped or needle-shaped. But when you look at an arborvitae tree (also called "northern white cedar"), you will find that its small, overlapping leaves are scale-shaped.

You may make a game of collecting cones of as many sorts as you can find. A good-sized arborvitae cone is only half an inch long. White-pine cones may be any length from five to ten inches. Perhaps you can find cones of all the different conifers mentioned in this book.

When most of the trees in a forest are cone-bearers, we call it a "coniferous forest." When most of the trees

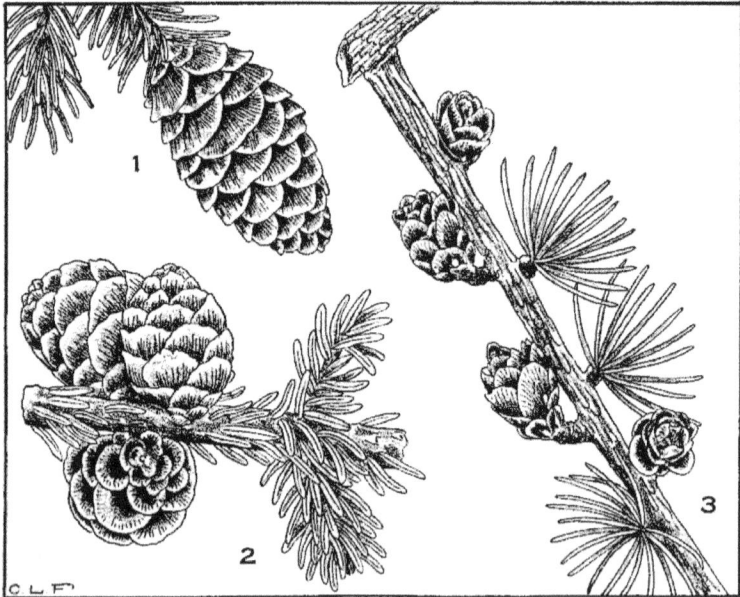

Cones and needles: 1—white spruce. 2—black spruce.
3—tamarack or larch.

around us have wide, thin leaves, we say we are in a "broadleaf forest." In some places, very often among hills, we may come into a "mixed forest"—with both conifers and broadleaf trees abundant.

A broadleaf tree does not bear its seeds in cones. The woody fruit of the alder, to be sure, may be said to be "conelike" in shape; but it differs from the true cones as you can see by comparing them. Some of the broadleaf trees you will find in the North Woods are oaks, maples, birches, beeches, and poplars. You would find it just as interesting to collect the seeds of these and other broadleaf trees as to collect cones. Their seeds vary greatly. For example, the oaks have nuts, or acorns; the maples have plump seeds with broad wings; the poplars have small seeds with cottony fluff that takes them sailing in the wind.

As we have remarked, all the conifers in the North Woods, except the tamarack, are evergreens. In these northern forests not one of the broadleaf trees is an evergreen.[1] Instead of staying green in the autumn, their wide, flat leaves turn yellow or red or brown and then flutter to the ground. Their bare branches wait until spring for a new set of leaves to make them green again.

Are you coming to the North Woods? When will your visit be?

AUTUMN . . . That is the gayest time, when the

---

[1] Some of the broadleaf trees, growing in parts of the country where the winters are not so severe, are evergreens, as you know if you are acquainted with live oaks and some of the hollies.

maple leaves glow with gorgeous reds and the beeches are clear yellow. The branches are bright overhead, but enough of the leaves have fallen to make your pathway brightly colored, too. As you walk along, perhaps you will find a place near Poplar Creek, where the beavers have been cutting a tree. So, of course, you plan to come back by moonlight, very quietly, in the hope of seeing them at work.

WINTER . . . If you enjoy a tramp on snowshoes, you may follow the tracks of the varying hare, or see what a ruffed grouse is eating for breakfast. As you pause to look at the evergreens with their boughs piled with fluffy snow, you notice how silent the woods seem. And then you hear a cheery voice greeting you. *"Chick-dee-dee,"* your little feathered neighbor calls, as he flies very near to see what you are doing. If you tie a chunk of suet to a branch, that will make a good Christmas feast for him.

SPRING . . . The colors of the broadleaf-tree tips are as varied in their springtime budding as they are in the fall. Not so bright and vivid, but their softer tints are fully as beautiful. The stay-in-the-North birds are singing their spring tunes; and the travel-to-the-South birds are coming back and singing, too. There is Seto, the redstart, just back from South America—and very glad he seems to be here. And there go two black-bear cubs out for a sunning and a frolic, with Mother Mah-kay near by to watch them. Feathery creatures and furry creatures, all are happy. The woodland stirs with the excitement of spring.

SUMMER . . . Of course, this is the time when most of you will come, for you have your longest vacations in summer. You may go to some parts of the North Woods in trains or on boats. You also may go in automobiles, for good roads now lead to many parts of the forest. Perhaps you will drive along one of these roads through a pine forest to a lake. A black bear, picking berries beside the highway, may stand up to watch you go by. A moose may walk across the road ahead of you. No one has ever harmed him, and he walks with such slow, unhurried steps that your driver may have to stop the car to wait for him to pass.

After you have reached your hotel or camp cabin or pitched your tent in the woods, you will start for a walk in the shade. If you have come from a part of the country where the weather is very hot in summer, you will be happy to feel the comfortable air. Perhaps your first thought will be, "Why, how *cool* the woods look— all the way from the ferns underfoot to the branches overhead!"

Weeks later, when your vacation is over and you come back from your last walk in the woods, what will you be thinking then? Very likely you will be saying to some comrade, "I hope people can always have forests. It is fun to hike and swim and watch the birds. Vacations could not be so jolly without woods like these. I hope a forest fire never spoils these trees."

And then you will remember that people are not the only creatures to enjoy the woodland. You will think of the furry and feathered dwellers there and add, "Yes, I hope these woods will always be here, so that the forest neighbors can have all the food and shelter that they need—in their own wilderness."

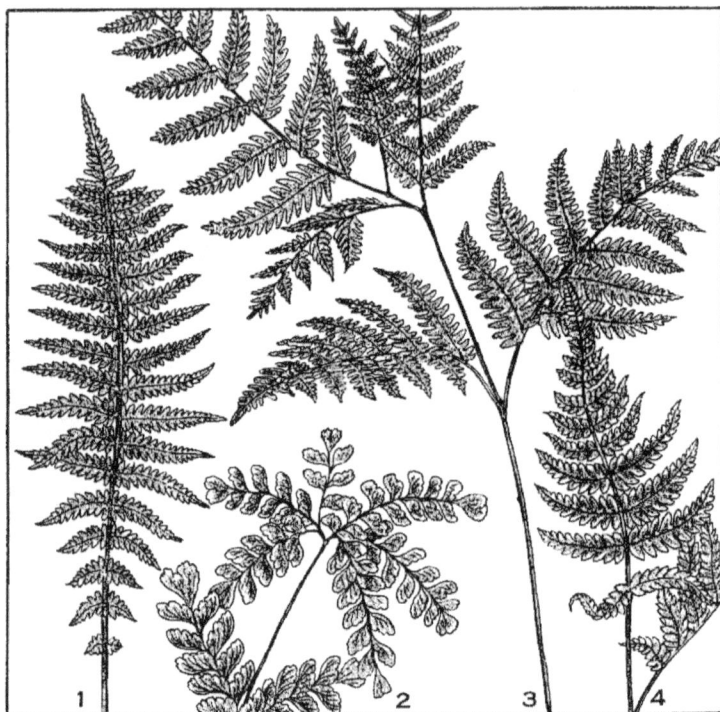

Some ferns that grow in the woodland: 1—wood fern, or New York fern. 2—maidenhair fern. 3—brake, or bracken. 4—beech fern.

CHAPTER II

THE HERD IN THE MOOSE YARD

THREE moose were tramping through their yard one cold January day. There was no fence around the yard, for it was not in a zoo, a park, or any other place where men put fences. There were no men with shovels in the yard either; and yet there were good paths through the deep snow. The paths led along sheltered slopes where poplars, willows, and birch saplings grew, and where tall thick pines served as windbreaks.

Alces and Moos-wa and Ten-nee, the three moose, made those paths themselves. Ten-nee, the calf, was not strong enough to do very much of the work; but he helped a little as he ran or walked along the paths, packing the snow with his hoofs as he went. In places, the snow was so deep that he could not see over the sides of the path. He walked between these high, white walls until he came to more open spaces where there were leafless twigs that he could chew and swallow. He liked the twigs of most of the bushes that grew there, and he browsed, too, on the low branches of poplars and birch trees; but he did not eat the pines.

Alces, the bull, and Moos-wa, the cow, kept these walks open. They began this work in November, when only a little snow covered the ground. Their big hoofs made long, pointed tracks in the snow. Alces' tracks were four inches wide, six inches long, and as much as five feet apart. Moos-wa's tracks were not quite so large and they were not quite so far apart, showing that her steps were shorter than those of her mate.

Moose tracks in the snow.

For a while, the moose could leave their paths when they wanted to go for walks through the forest. But when snows became deep, they could not do that. Instead, they stayed in their "yard." They would not leave it again until springtime, when the thick drifts of snow would melt.

The moose did not mind staying at home. Indeed, no moose travels far unless hunters or wolves chase him or fire follows him. Alces had lived in the forest eight years, yet he never had been ten miles from the

Alces, the bull moose, stood beside the lake
and gave a loud bellow.

shore of Walloon's lake. In the fall, he often crossed low ridges to lakes a few miles away; and once he had gone a bit farther. That was when an old bear came to live in the cedar woods near the lake shore. But when the bear disappeared, Alces returned to the very place where he and Moos-wa later made their yard.

The moose yard was in a low, damp valley half a mile from the lake. Balsam firs and white cedars grew near it. There also were thickets of small trees, or large shrubs, called striped maple or moosewood, and growths of willows, poplars, and birches. Alces and Ten-nee ate twigs and buds of all these except the white cedars. They especially liked the moosewood. Their best, most-used paths were those that led to moosewood thickets.

Until the snow became too deep, they also ate sedges and marsh grass. When those were covered, they found some plants called "horsetails" with tips above the snow, and ate them. The jointed stems of the horsetails were tough and harsh, but they tasted good enough to the moose. They were better to eat than the club moss which was abundant in the forest, though the old moose sometimes ate that, too.[2]

When you look at the picture of Alces, you may think he used his large antlers to shovel snow from deep drifts, or to brush it from branches of balsam fir.

---

[2] Other names for "horsetails" are *Equisetum* and *scouring-rush.* They are small relatives of plants as big as trees that lived in forests and swamps of the Coal Age, millions of years ago. Club mosses also are dwarf relatives of Coal Age plants which were tall trees. These plants are mentioned in "Finding Rocks," a chapter in *Surprises* and in "Materials and Devices for Cleaning," a chapter in *Science at Home.*

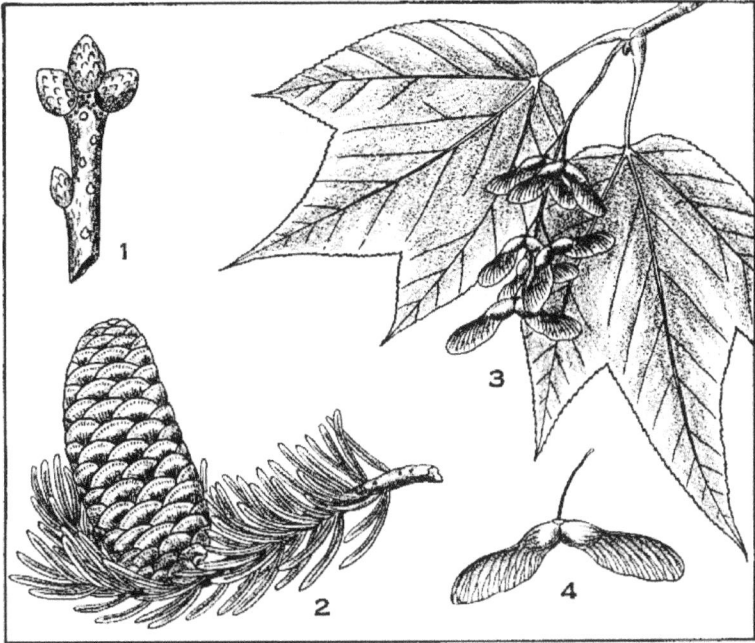

The moose often went to balsam fir and moosewood for food.

1—tender twig-tip and buds of a balsam fir. 2—balsam fir needles and cone. 3—leaves and seeds of the striped maple, or moosewood. 4—moosewood seeds, with wide "wings."

They do look as if they might be handy for work of that sort. However, Alces had no such help from his antlers. Indeed, he was without them for most of the winter. He shed them in December. When he did have them, he wore these antlers for weapons and not shovels!

As you may know, the solid antlers of moose, caribou, wapiti, and other members of the Deer Family, are quite different from the hollow horns that certain other hoofed animals have. Antelopes, bison, cattle, goats, and sheep do not shed their hollow horns; but the animals with solid antlers shed them every year and then grow new ones.

The bull moose's new antlers began to grow in April of each year. While they were growing, they were covered with deep, velvety skin in which rich blood was flowing. This blood held lime and other minerals that made the antlers grow rapidly. During this time of growth, they were tender, and Alces was careful not to hit them against branches. In about three months, however, his antlers were full-grown and hard. Then the "velvet" dried and came off in shreds. At first the fresh, bare antlers were bony white, but by fall they were tanned to a deep brown except that the tips were white and polished from being rubbed against bushes and trees.

While his antlers were growing and becoming hard, Alces lived alone. He spent spring and early summer on the ridges that were covered with willow and poplar thickets. These thickets became very hot in August, while millions of flies buzzed through them. So many flies bit Alces' big, soft nose that he moved to more open woods near the lake. If flies and heat bothered him there, he could bathe in the lake water.

Though Alces knew nothing about a clock, he divided his August days into six separate parts quite regularly. Before dawn, he got up and went to the lake, where he waded and ate a breakfast of water-lily leaves. At sunrise he went back to the woods and lay down, sleeping or chewing his cud until about eleven o'clock. Then he waded, bathed, and spent three hours among the plants near the lake's edge, where he ate his dinner. He took a nap from two until half-past five. Then he ate a supper of lily stems, grass, sedge, and horsetails. If the day was very hot, he bathed. At dark, he went back to the woods to chew his cud and sleep until morning, when he began all over again.

In September, Alces changed his ways. He became restless, trotting through the woods and hitting bushes with his antlers. Often he stamped his feet and gave deep, rumbling grunts. His temper became bad, too. He chased harmless young moose away, and scared off deer that passed through the woods.

One night, Alces stamped his way to the shore of the lake. There he lifted his head proudly and gave a hoarse, grunting bellow.

A young moose heard the deep, roaring sound. If he had been as old and strong and brave as Alces, he would have bellowed loudly in reply. Then he would have gone to meet Alces and the two bulls would have clashed their antlers together and fought. But the young bull was only three years old. The heavy voice of Alces made him timid. He slipped off among the pine trees, glad to get away.

There was no old bull in the valley to challenge Alces and become his rival. But Alces had one answer to his call. Moos-wa was walking in the moonlight with young Ten-nee when she heard Alces bellow. She liked the roaring sound of his voice. She was feeling rather lonely and called softly, "Whoowah."

Moos-wa and Ten-nee at the edge of their winter yard.

Alces heard Moos-wa and went to meet her. He was lonesome, too, and was glad to find her.

Ten-nee was wary of the big bull at first and stayed away for a few days. Then he came back to Moos-wa and found that Alces was kind to him. So he followed the two moose when Alces led his mate to the shallow lake where they waded in above their knees to feed on yellow pond lilies called "spatterdocks." There were no flowers on the lily plants then, but the moose liked the thick, pulpy leaves and the tender stems. They went into the lake every day for food until the weather became so cold that ice formed on the water. After that it was not long before snow began to fall, and the herd of three moose went to live in their winter yard.

No other moose joined Alces, Moos-wa and Ten-nee in their winter home that year. Their nearest neighbors were a few snowshoe rabbits, two squirrels, a porcupine, and some Canada Jays.[3]

The Canada Jays visited the moose yard very often. They sometimes found boring insects in the dead branches that the moose knocked down and broke as they tramped about. These birds have a habit of lingering near moose yards; and for this reason people call them "moose birds."

When Alces dropped his antlers, the squirrels and porcupine nibbled them. The squirrels feasted during the daytime; and the porcupine came at night and

---

[3] A Canada Jay is very closely related to the Rocky Mountain Jay, which you may read more about in "Two Jays and a Nutcracker," a chapter in *Mountain Neighbors*.

stayed almost till daybreak. When these little animals finally finished their antler picnics, there were only two rough stubs left.

But Alces did not care what happened to these old things he had shed. He could grow new ones when he needed them. Until that time, he had enough to do breaking paths, without carrying two great, heavy antlers on his shaggy head.

CHAPTER III

NAK-KEE AND THE
SNOWSHOE HARE

A Red Fox and His Mate

NAK-KEE, the red fox, lived on a rocky ridge north of Walloon's lake. That ridge once was covered with a thick forest of spruces, pines, and firs. Years before Nak-kee was born, however, lightning started a fire that burned all the large evergreens. Poplars and maples grew in their place, with willows in several damp ravines. Their leaves made shade during the summer, but changed color and fell when autumn came. In winter, sunshine could reach every part of the maple and poplar groves.

The sun warmed some big gray and reddish-brown boulders that lay on one slope of the hill. Among them was something that looked like a stone of a different shade—rather a yellowish red. But a chickadee, coming near, was not fooled. He knew too much to perch on Nak-kee, even if the fox lay as still as a stone when he curled up for an afternoon nap.

But didn't Nak-kee feel cold, sleeping out of doors in winter? Well, of course he sought his den when he needed it; but now the sun on his fur coat was keeping him warm. Besides, he had a good muffler which he wrapped around his front paws and face. This muffler was his fluffy tail. He could see through the edge of it and breathe through it, but it kept his nose and eyes from getting chilly.

Nak-kee's eyes opened as the chickadee came close. But the little bird would not disturb him, and it was too clever to be caught. Nak-kee shut his eyes and had another nap.

He awoke with a start, and stood up quickly. That *thump thump!* was made by Wah-boos, a snowshoe rabbit,[4] hopping among the stones. Rabbit meat is good food. Many men like to eat it when it is well cooked. Nak-kee liked it, too. So did Cheesay, the lynx, and several other forest dwellers who never bothered to cook their food. So Nak-kee was ready to chase that rabbit—but Wah-boos saw and smelled the fox just in time. He dashed away in long hops, so fast that he was soon out of sight. Nak-kee yawned and sat down. No use chasing a rabbit with such a good start as that!

Well, perhaps he could find a grouse. Men had not been hunting at that edge of the forest; and there might be some of these birds not far away. The red fox started off to hunt.

When he came to a big, fallen log, he jumped up and ran along it, leaving tracks in the snow there. These tracks looked very much like those a small dog would

---

[4]A snowshoe rabbit is also known by the name of "varying hare." There is a chapter about "Little Snowshoes" in *Holiday Hill.*

Nak-Kee the Red Fox

have made. This is not strange, since foxes belong to the Dog Family.

Suddenly, Nak-kee made a sidewise jump to the ground and pounced upon a little mound in the snow. Two ruffed grouse were sleeping under that mound. One managed to fly away, but Nak-kee ate the other one for the first course of his dinner.

Nak-kee started out to hunt.

Nak-kee was not nearly so hungry as he had been, but he went on with his hunt, poking his nose into every thicket he came to, and listening in every hollow. In one hollow he heard a mouse running in a tunnel under the snow. With a quick snap of his jaws, the fox caught it. He found mice about as good to eat as hares and grouse—only it took a dozen of them to make a meal.

Next, Nak-kee trotted down the ridge. He stopped to sniff at a stump which foxes used for their signals.

Odors told him that his mate had been there not long before. If he hurried, he would catch up with her. Nak-kee barked *"Yap-yap-yap!"* sharply and hastened along her trail.

His mate heard those three barks, and sat down for a few minutes. Then she got up and walked on slowly, waiting for Nak-kee to come.

He found her just at the edge of a mountain-maple thicket. The two foxes looked at each other and sniffed. Nak-kee rubbed his mate's black nose. She snapped playfully and jumped away, while Nak-kee trotted around her and nipped at her bushy tail. Soon both foxes were romping as if they still were puppies.

WAH-BOOS, THE SNOWSHOE HARE

While the foxes were frolicking near the mountain maples, Wah-boos, the hare, rested beside the willows. As he twitched his ears, their black tips showed plainly. The rest of his body was as white as the snow on which he was sitting. A hawk, overhead, that did not see his ears, thought he was just a lump of snow, fallen from one of the trees.

Wah-boos saw the hawk, however, and he sat very, very still. In fact, he hardly took a deep breath until the big, hungry bird disappeared. Then he sat up, shook his head, and hopped toward a slope near the thicket.

As he hopped, Wah-boos showed why men call him a "snowshoe rabbit." His feet were broad, with wide-spreading toes. They also were covered with long, stiff

Wah-boos sat beside the willows,
sniffing and twitching his ears.

hairs which spread out like the "webs" of snowshoes. Even where the snow was soft, Wah-boos could hop along on it without sinking. Where the snow was firm, he could travel across it just as well as if it were bare, hard ground.

There were times when those "snowshoes" meant a great deal to Wah-boos. Just then, for example, as he glanced back up the slope, he caught sight of two red foxes. Nak-kee and his mate had stopped playing and were now hunting together. They were very near Wah-boos, as they crept past some bushes bent over by the snow. The hare squeaked with surprise as he jumped away. His very first leap was eight feet long, and he landed with a hard *thud!* But his big, hairy feet kept him from sinking—and away he went in another leap. In three minutes, he had left the foxes far behind, and was sitting among tangled gooseberry and blackberry stems under two fallen trees. He felt safe there, for he knew that no hunting fox would follow him into that prickly retreat.

Tangles which stopped lynxes and foxes did not bother Wah-boos at all. He could jump at almost full speed through thickets of willows which were only four inches apart. He could hop over some branches, slip under others, and twist around jagged snags. He once squeezed through a three-inch crack between logs. Some of his fur caught on their bark, but his skin was not even scratched.

Those logs were in the very thicket near which Wah-boos sat when he saw the hawk. The hillside where he had just left the foxes was not far from that same thicket. The two fallen trees where he was hiding were in the woods at the foot of the hill. Wah-boos did not know what was beyond the woods. Though he was a full-grown hare, he never had gone away from the hill, the woods, and the willow thickets—all of which took up about thirty acres of the forest. Why should he go somewhere else, when they gave him everything he needed?

Though Wah-boos was a stay-at-home, he wasn't lonely or unfriendly. No other snowshoe rabbit lived in *exactly* his thirty acres, but there were many whose homes overlapped part of his. Wah-boos met one of these neighbors that evening after he left his prickly hiding place and hopped among the willows. They wriggled their noses and sniffed a greeting. Then they went to a place where the willow shoots were young and tender, with good-tasting bark. Both rabbits ate the bark for supper. For dessert, they nibbled some wisps of dry grass that stuck up through the snow.

The sun was setting when they began to eat; there was moonlight when they stopped. As the moon came in sight, three other rabbits hopped to a clear place at the edge of the thicket. One of them found a hard bit of icy snow and tapped it with her front feet. That seemed to be a signal. In a moment a big rabbit jumped toward her, and the two began to play tag among the trees. Two others started to hop in circles, jumping over low bushes and logs. When one of them jumped straight into the air, the other rabbit dodged under him and managed to get ahead.

Wah-boos watched while the other rabbits played.

Wah-boos did not join the play for a long time. He hopped to the edge of the thicket and sat up very stiff and straight. He looked, sniffed, and wriggled his ears. He was watching, smelling, and listening for creatures that might try to slip up and catch one of his happy friends.

Nothing came, but Wah-boos kept on watching. After a while, he noticed that the rabbit who had thumped the snow was leaving her game of tag. She hopped to the foot of a berry bush, and sat up just as Wah-boos was sitting. In a moment, she also began to look, sniff, and listen. She was ready to take her turn at keeping watch.

When Wah-boos saw what she was doing, he took a long jump and landed cheerfully just in front of one of the tag-players. The tag-player dodged; and Wah-boos kicked snow on his nose and jumped across a wide stone. That seemed to mean "I am 'it,' " for the other rabbit tried to catch him. Jump, *thump,* jump they went over logs and around bushes, leaving broad tracks in the snow, but never breaking through it.

Snowshoe-feet were good for escaping danger. And they also were good for play on a pleasant, moonlit night!

CHAPTER IV

CHEESAY, THE LYNX

CHEESAY opened his yellow eyes and yawned. He stretched lazily as he glanced at the ceiling of his home in the midst of the forest. He saw above him the big trunk of a fallen pine tree. The snow had piled against it in drifts, making thick walls for the narrow room in which Cheesay lay.

Neither the cold wind nor the brightest winter sunlight could get through the fallen trunk and the drifted snow. This was just the sort of dark, safe shelter that Cheesay found comfortable. He had been sleeping there most of the day and it was now time for him to waken.

For Cheesay, like many other forest dwellers, went to bed early in the morning and did not usually get up until sunset. By that time he began to feel hungry, though he seldom went out to hunt for a meal until the forest became quite dark. He could see at night even better than he could in the daytime.

When the sunlight at last disappeared, Cheesay stepped out of his home. He looked like a shadow moving slowly across the snow. The fur on his body was long and fluffy; and its colors were a mixture of pale gray, white, black, and brown. His face was light gray, with bushy side whiskers that made it seem very broad; and his furry ears had long, black tips. These tips flopped a little when Cheesay jumped over fallen logs or made other quick movements.

He was three feet long, with a stubby four-inch tail whose tip was black all the way round. Because of this short tail, some people called Cheesay a "bobcat," though that name belongs to a relative whose tail (six or seven inches long) is not black all the way round the tip, but is white underneath.

Both lynxes and bobcats belong to the Cat Family and both are often called "wildcats." You could have guessed, after seeing him, that Cheesay was a relative of a common house cat, in spite of his very long legs, very big feet, and very short tail.

Though Cheesay weighed almost forty pounds, he did not break through the soft snow. He did not sink in and have to wade. This was because his big feet were covered with pads of stiff hairs. They spread out and acted like broad snowshoes that woodsmen wear when they walk through the forest in winter.[5]

When the hungry lynx came to a clearing, he stopped and crouched in the snow.

Then he stood up, took a long jump, and trotted swiftly across the open space. He did not like broad clearings one bit better than he liked daylight. (Only

[5] In this connection, you may like to read "Snowshoes," a chapter in *Through Four Seasons*.

Cheesay's bushy side whiskers made his face seem very broad.

once in his whole life did he ever really leave the forest. That was when a fire drove him away. Cheesay had run ahead of the fire, into an open treeless country. But he did not feel at home there, and hurried on to another forest just as soon as he could.)

As Cheesay left the clearing and entered the woods again, he began to walk slowly. He kept his yellow eyes wide open, and noticed many interesting things. He came to a "yard" among some birch trees where moose had stood while they ate twigs. He saw a fir tree that had been scratched by bears. He found a hemlock whose bark had been peeled by hungry porcupines. The peeled places were yellowish white and shiny. Cheesay circled round and round them and came quite close to get a better look. He was so curious about those bright spots that he did not leave them to chase a rabbit who jumped up from the snow and hurried away as fast as his long hind legs could take him.

Perhaps it was the scent of the fleeing rabbit, however, that reminded Cheesay how hungry he was. He had hunting habits that were much like those of a common cat, and the same sort of appetite. He liked mice and birds when he could catch them, as well as does his tame relative. But it was not a mouse nor a bird that he hunted that night.

Within a few moments, he entered a growth of white cedars, crept among them very slowly, and then made a sudden dash. Soon he was enjoying a meal of rabbit meat. When one rabbit was eaten, he caught another. Two rabbits made a good supper, even for a hungry lynx. Really, it was breakfast and dinner, too,

Cheesay crouched in the snow.

for Cheesay seemed to be quite contented with one big meal a day.

Still, when a third rabbit hopped close to him, Cheesay could not bear to waste the chance. He caught it with one big paw. Then he carried it to the side of a fallen log and hid it under the snow. He could keep this meat there in cold storage just as well as men can keep meat in a refrigerator. Some night, rabbits might be hard to catch. Then he could come to his snow pantry and help himself to at least half a meal.

That task over, Cheesay sat down on the snow. He licked his paws, washed his face, and cleaned the long bristles of his mustache. He even gave a few hoarse purrs, as a pet cat does, when he has eaten heartily and is ready to take a nap.

But Cheesay did not go to sleep—he could rest enough in the daytime. He trotted up a slanting log and jumped off; came back to the log and jumped again. Then he tried a third time, leaping through the air. He landed in the snow, twelve feet away. Even this did not seem far enough, so he leaped once more. This jump took him fifteen feet, and Cheesay broke through the surface of the snow when he came down on it. He pulled his furry feet out, shook them, and walked toward a clump of pine trees.

When he reached them, Cheesay began to mew. His mews became louder and louder; and at last turned into screeches. This noise woke many sleeping birds, made rabbits go into hiding, and sounded very, very fierce. Yet Cheesay did not feel fierce at all. He was well fed, happy, and ready to play. Those screeches were meant for invitations to other lynxes to come and play with him.

Two of Cheesay's neighbors felt playful, too. They met near a pine tree, looked at each other for a moment, and walked side by side through the woods. When they found Cheesay, they took a few long leaps; and then all three animals began to play. They chased one another among the trees, jumped over fallen logs, and twisted and dodged between snowy bushes. Though they did not touch each other for "tag," they seemed to take turns being "it." They acted like huge, fluffy, short-tailed kittens, and seemed just as happy as kittens ever are in their rough-and-tumble games.

When the lynxes grew tired of playing, they parted without saying good-by. One of Cheesay's guests took an extra long leap and bounded away across the snow. The other found the trail of a grouse and followed it through the woods. They left Cheesay standing on a boulder among the snowy pines.

He did not seem surprised nor offended when his playmates hurried away. He jumped a few times, just for fun, and knocked the snow from two low branches. Then he began to walk up the valley that led to his log-and-snow-covered home.

Before he had gone very far, Cheesay met a porcupine. It stopped, stuck its nose between its paws, and rattled its sharp, barbed spines. Cheesay sat down on the snow to watch it. Twice he reached out a big, furry paw—but drew it back very quickly. Once, when he was very young, Cheesay had touched a porcupine. A quill stuck into his paw and stayed there for a long time before it worked its way out. Cheesay never forgot the hurt caused by that quill. Never again would he make the mistake of petting a porcupine!

Since that spiny creature was not much fun to watch, the big lynx soon left it and trotted up the valley. He stopped for a moment to sniff the trail of a skunk, but decided not to follow it.

At the tracks of a fox, however, Cheesay turned and hurried across the snow. Lynxes and foxes have fights, much as some cats and dogs do. But Cheesay didn't even meet this fox. This bushy-tailed creature dodged into a hollow log, just before the lynx caught up with him. Cheesay tried to follow, but the tunnel in the old log was too small for his body. He clawed and snarled at the opening for ten minutes before he found that his work was useless. Then he gave up his attempt, turned without a sound, and went home.

The sky was becoming blue when Cheesay reached his den. He sniffed a few times to make sure that all was well; and followed his own big footprints around and around the log. By that time he began to feel lazy. He went into his bedroom, sat down, and gave his face another washing. Then he tucked his feet under his long fur, and settled himself in the darkest corner for a rest.

When night came once more, Cheesay would go out to find supper, sing, and play with his neighbors. Until then he would sleep, hidden from all the forest creatures that liked to work and play by daylight.

CHAPTER V

THE WHITE-TAILED DEER

WHITE-TAIL stopped near a meadow in the forest. Bears sometimes came there to hunt mice or eat berries. White-tail had seen them there, so now he looked and listened carefully. He saw no bears; and all he could hear was dry grass, rattling in the breeze. He signaled to Wabai, his mate, who was waiting with her two young ones, or fawns. The signal meant "All is well, follow me." When the fawns rubbed noses instead of coming, he gave a second signal that meant "Hurry!"

White-tail sent that message without making a sound. He just lifted his tail, held it upward, and then let it drop. When his tail was up, its long, white hairs showed plainly, though the woods were almost dark. They made a very good signal. They also showed how White-tail got his name, though some persons liked to call him the "bannertail," or Virginia, deer.

Father White-tail did not care about names. He wanted to lead his family to their beds in a thicket of young spruce trees. He hurried across the meadow and took a short cut through a swamp where there were many dead, fallen cedar trees. If the fawns lagged or tried to play, he looked back and lifted his tail in the "Hurry!" signal.

The beds to which the deer were going would not look very good to us. They were just bare, gravelly places on the ground, in a thicket of black spruce saplings. But White-tail, Wabai and the fawns thought they were very good. They did not need to have their beds lined with moss, grass, and leaves.

White-tail awoke very early next morning, long before the sun came up. He lay still, with his eyes open. Then he got up, stretched his hind legs, and wriggled his tail. He also grunted a few times before he walked away through the woods. He could hear Wabai getting up. She and the fawns trotted after him. Soon the whole deer family was going single file through the woods.

The deer stopped at a clump of red-oak trees whose acorns had dropped to the ground. White-tail thought that acorns were better than any other food. Wabai and the fawns thought so, too. They ate every one they could find. When they still were hungry, they nibbled some twigs of dwarf birch and the tips of leatherwood bushes.

Snowflakes began to fall while the deer were eating. Snow fell still faster when they went for a drink. The flakes came *pat, pat* on the spruce needles as White-tail led his family to their beds. By suppertime, the storm was so heavy that the deer went only a little way for food. The fawns were glad to turn back and lie down in a sheltered place close to their mother.

Snow fell until midnight, but morning came clear and sunny. White-tail did not wait for the snow to melt.

White-tail paused while he looked and listened.

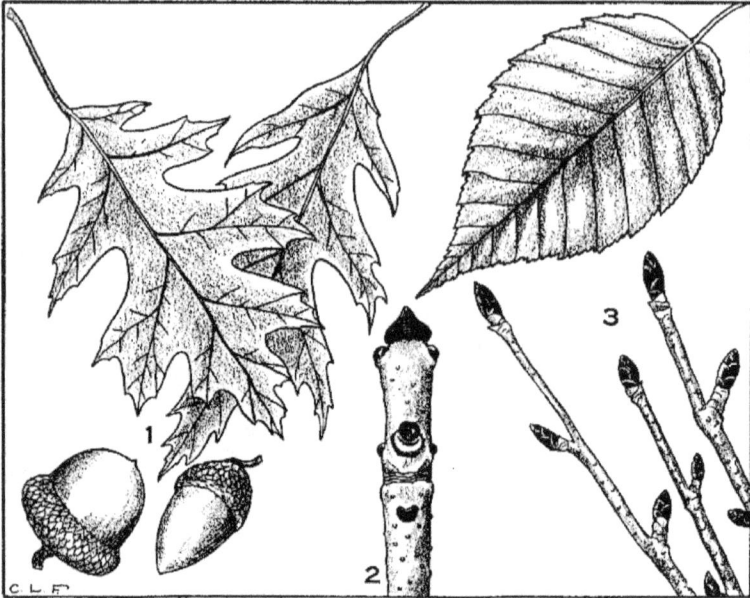

*Food for White-tail deer: 1—leaves and acorns of red oaks;
White-tail eats the acorns. 2—a tender twig of green ash.
3—leaf and winter twigs of the yellow birch. White-tail likes
the twigs, with their pointed buds.*

Before sunrise, he got up, grunted, and started toward
the oak grove. He dragged his toes just a bit in the snow,
but Wabai lifted her feet above it. The fawns lifted their
feet so high that they looked as if they were walking
on stilts. They never had seen snow before this storm.
They were not sure they liked this strange, cold, white
stuff that covered the branches and the ground!

White-tail was very handsome as he walked
through the woods. He was even more handsome
when he trotted with his white tail held up straight.
He was most handsome of all when he ran. Then he

kept his head high, too. Instead of galloping evenly, like a horse, he took three or four low, springy bounds and then jumped high in the air. After this, came more low bounds, another leap, and so on. Wabai ran in the same way, and the fawns did their best to keep up with her and White-tail.

Although White-tail seemed very proud, he did not know what important creatures he and his kind really were. Many animals have become rare as North America was settled. Others have gone to live in remote, hard-to-reach places. Some have become extinct—we must go to museums and look at mounted specimens if we wish to see them.

Although white-tail deer are placed in museums, we do not need to go there to see them. They have not become rare, and they do not hide in distant places. They live in woods and swamps from Mexico and Florida to Quebec and westward to the Rocky Mountains of Canada. Sometimes half a dozen white-tail deer will live about a swamp pond not far from a farmhouse. They like woods that have been cut and are now growing up again. They also like the thickets that grow after forest fires kill pines, hemlocks, and other big trees. Then, too, they like places cleared in forests by men for barnyards, pastures, and fields. That seems to be the reason white-tail deer have followed human settlers into swampy parts of Manitoba, and into forests of Quebec, New Brunswick, and other parts of Canada. They have been going farther and farther and perhaps they will not stop till they reach Hudson Bay.

White-tail, himself, knew nothing about all his relatives in different parts of the United States and Canada. His attention was centered on his own family.

After the first November storm, the snow melted very quickly. Snow water, mixed with soil, made mud in which the deer family left their tracks. The fawns made dainty, pointed footprints, with the toes very close together. White-tail's toes spread a bit and the marks which they made were more than three inches long. When he ran, the tracks spread still more widely and showed traces of the two little hoofs behind the big ones on which he stepped.

While the weather stayed warm, the deer ate every acorn they could find. The acorns made them fat, healthy, and strong. This acorn fat would help them through the cold winter weather.

Later came a spell when snow fell almost every day. It covered the slopes where acorns lay, and piled in deep drifts on the meadow. Both White-tail and Wabai hunted for places where the tall grass was not quite covered, or where there were bushes whose tips were good to eat. The old deer also trampled down trails for the fawns, whose legs were not yet long enough to go through the deepest snow.

Other deer were doing the same thing. Soon they began to stay in the sheltered part of the forest where White-tail and his family found food. They used his trails, making them wider; he used theirs when he wanted to. All the deer made new beds and new paths which crisscrossed one another among drifts of snow.

These crisscross paths formed a "deer yard." The yard belonged to White-tail, Wabai, the fawns, and all their friends who had helped make it. In fact, all those deer joined in a herd. It was very much like a big family gathering.

Did White-tail lead the herd? No, he didn't. Even before new deer came to the yard, White-tail stopped guiding the fawns and giving signals to Wabai. Instead, she often gave signals to him—and often she was the first one to break a trail to some new, good food. In time, she even led the whole herd, if the herd really needed leading. Most of the time, however, each deer did as he pleased, eating, walking, sleeping, or playing among the tangle of trails.

Several more deer moved into the yard in December, long after Wabai, White-tail, and their friends had tramped out most of the yard. One of the newcomers was almost as large as White-tail. He had big antlers that turned forward in graceful curves and had fourteen branches, or "points." White-tail's antlers had only twelve points—yet even they were much more handsome than the antlers of an ordinary deer.

Though their yard had no signs saying **KEEP OUT**, the deer did not want everyone in it. When a fox slipped in, they snorted and shook their heads angrily. As he began to follow the fawns, Wabai stood behind them and struck at him with her sharp hoofs. The fox dodged and snapped at her—but just then White-tail ran up, followed by the buck with big antlers. Helping each other, they chased the fox up one trail and down

The new deer had handsome antlers.

another, turning him back when he tried to dodge. After ten minutes of that, the fox was glad to find a place where he could jump from the trail to a snowdrift and run away through the woods.

The two big deer watched him go, holding their heads very proudly. They seemed to say, "We are friends—and see what we did to a meat-eating beast that didn't belong in our home!"

CHAPTER VI

TRAVELERS AND STAY-AT-HOMES

SETO was glad when he reached the northern forest. He perched on a twig and sang *"Che-wee, che-ser-wee"* quickly and happily. Then he spread his wings and tail, dancing a fluttering little dance. The flaming orange-red patches on his black wings and tail showed while he danced. Now and then he would dart into the air, as if he were catching insects.

Like the other redstarts, Seto had made a long journey. His winter home was in Venezuela, a country in the northern part of South America. There he hunted insects in big ceiba trees, or fluttered about bamboo thickets. When there were hard rains (which was very often, indeed), he hid under the leaves of palms. These leaves made a good umbrella. Seto liked them for a sunshade, too, when he became too hot in the bright sunshine.

When March came, Seto and his red-and-black redstart friends left the woods of Venezuela. They flew across the Isthmus of Panama, and northward to

Seta and Seto Redstart perched in a hemlock tree.

Mexico. On the way, they met many other redstarts, who had spent their winter in Central America. They made large flocks when they gathered in the woods of Yucatan.

One morning, Seto's flock left the woods of Yucatan. They flew along the shore for a while. Then they turned and crossed the Gulf of Mexico, traveling high in the air with the water far below them. They kept on going until they saw a grove in Louisiana, where there were big oaks. The branches of these oaks were draped with the long threadlike stems and threadlike leaves of a strange gray plant called "long moss," or "Spanish moss," although it really is not a moss at all.

The birds rested a few hours in the Louisiana grove and then traveled northward. Sometimes they flew one hundred miles or more, without pausing to eat. At other times, they often stopped to play in pasture thickets or among the trees in towns. The middle of May came before the first redstarts reached their forest in the North.

Seto arrived so early that he had to wait several days for his mate, Seta, to come. Other redstarts were waiting, too. Everyone that Seto could see was a male bird colored as he was: mostly black, with white on the underside between the black breast and tail; and with bright orange-red patches on the sides of the breast, on the wings, and on the tail. Each had stiff bristles about the mouth, looking like a little mustache.

Seto spent his days of waiting quite happily—singing

and catching insects. Part of the time he seemed to be just playing.

While he played, Seto met other birds that lived in the forest. One of them was Jack, the Canada Jay, whose nest had been built before the redstarts left South America. His children were already able to take care of themselves. They often hunted food in the hemlock tree where Seto liked to perch. Jack and his mate had not needed to take much of a journey before they nested. They lived in the Land of Snows all winter, as did the ruffed grouse and the great horned owls.

Other stay-at-home forest birds were the brown-capped chickadees and the black-capped chickadees. Chickadees of both sorts spent the winter in Seto's forest. Like Jack, the Canada Jay, they did not need to leave the Land of Snows during the cold months. They even sang when there were snowstorms. The blackcaps sang *"Chick, dee, dee"* quite sweetly; and the browncaps sang *"Tsick, chee, day-day"* in thin, drawling voices. In some parts of the North Woods, browncaps and blackcaps both built their nests. But most of the browncaps went farther north for their summer homes than blackcaps ever go.[6]

When spring came, and the ash trees began to blossom, the browncaps had a pretty warbling tune to sing, though they sometimes said *"Tch-chip!"* very loudly. Two of them were tumbling about some branches

---

[6] More is told about black-capped chickadees in "Chick D. D," a chapter in *Bird Stories.*

The Chickadees were stay-at-home birds.

and calling "*Tch-chip!*" to each other when Seto's mate arrived from the South.

Seta, and the redstarts who were her traveling companions, did not wear black and orange-red suits like Seto's. Seta was pale yellow where Seto was bright red, while her gray and olive-green feathers covered most of the places where his feathers were black. Seta, however, wore mustache bristles like Seto's. (*Seta*, by the way, is a Latin word meaning "bristle," or "stiff hair." So, perhaps, "Seta" and "Seto" are good enough names for redstarts with mustaches.)

Her different colors did not bother Seta. She did not need flashing bright trimmings to make her happy. She was content to play with her gayer mate. She perched on the twig of a swamp maple, or red maple tree, while Seto did his prettiest fluttering dance on a branch not far away. Then both birds dodged about some young hemlocks, hurried past a patch of wild gooseberries, and perched on a mountain-maple tree, which was not much larger than a shrub. Seto did his dance again on the branches of this small maple.

On the next day, Seta began to build her nest. She put it in a mountain-ash tree that was less than fifteen feet high. This tree grew on a rocky hillside where there were only a few pines but quite a number of small broadleaf trees. Seto had chosen this hillside before Seta came, but he let her select the tree in which the nest was to be built. Meanwhile, he kept other redstarts away from the hillside. He had to flash his tail, wave his wings, sing, and even do a bit of fighting to keep

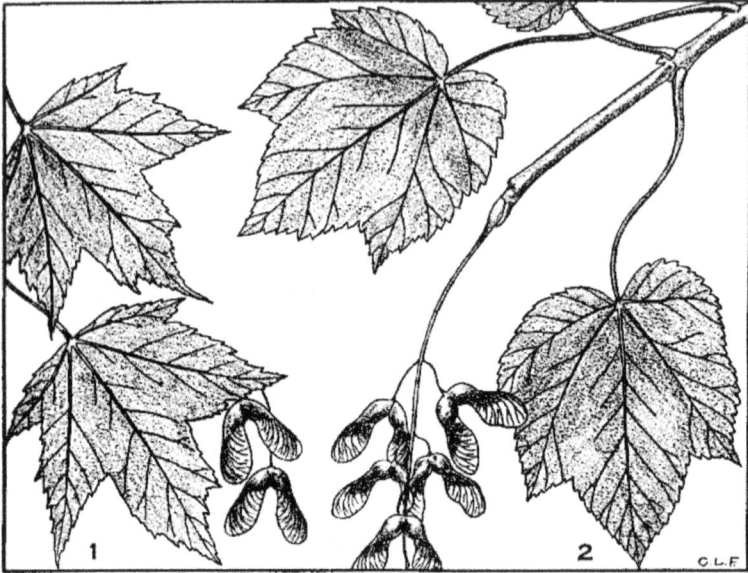

Two of the maples which grow in the North Woods:
1—leaves and seeds of the red maple, or swamp maple.
2—leaves and seeds of a mountain maple.

them from settling in the region that he had picked for his own home. He did not wish the company of his traveling comrades then—Seta was company enough.

While Seto kept other birds away, Seta built the nest herself. She used strips of tough inner bark, wisps of dried grass, cobwebs, and last year's silk from fireweed seeds. She wove them into a deep, round cup which was higher than it was wide.

Since Seta did not work all day long, she took a week to build her nest. The last thing she did to it was to fix a lining of dried grass roots and other fine fibers.

When the nest was finished, Seta laid four

creamy-white eggs. Each egg had purplish and brown spots at its larger end.

Seto had not helped with the nest-building, and he did not sit on the eggs. He did not even bring food to his mate, so she had to go and catch her own. On warm days, that was easy. On cold ones, Seta stayed on the nest as long as she could, and hurried back after eating. Even so, the eggs became quite cool before she covered them again. Yet, after twelve days they hatched into four healthy, hungry little redstarts.

As soon as that happened, Seto set to work. He flew from branch to branch of the maples, poked about the gooseberry bushes, and searched every mountain-ash stem. As soon as he filled his beak with insects, he carried them to the four babies and then went to other trees and bushes to hunt again. He brought caterpillars— both hairy and naked kinds. He found leaf-hoppers and young leaf-eating beetles by the hundreds. Then, for a change, he snapped gnats from the air, and snatched flies that hummed to and fro. He worked so busily that Seta sometimes had little to do except to catch her own food.

With so much to eat, the little redstarts grew very fast and were soon able to leave the nest. First, they perched on branches while Seto and Seta brought insects to them. Next, they began to flutter about. Then, they started to fly and catch insects for themselves. By mid-July, they did all their own hunting—none needed to sit and wait for Father Seto or Mother Seta to bring food.

One morning, rather early in August, this whole family of six redstarts gathered in a mountain-maple shrub. They called *"Ching, ching!"* as they hopped quickly from twig to twig. In answer to their call, other redstarts came to join them. Seto did not object. He no longer needed his hillside for a private hunting ground. Indeed, he was not going to stay there any longer. He called *"Ching!"* quite sharply and dashed up into the air.

Seta joined him in a moment, and after her came their children. Other redstarts followed; and soon all were flying southward in a zigzag, broken line. They flew until early afternoon, when they stopped for a picnic luncheon of insects. Then they began to fly again.

The hillside where Seta had built her nest in the North Woods was already far behind them. The redstart travelers were on their southward way. And on their fall trip the male birds with bright orange-red flash colors did not go by themselves. They went in company with the mothers and all the young redstarts.

This long journey would take the birds back to the bamboo thickets of their winter home. And people who saw Seto in South America would not call him by his English name of "Redstart." They would speak of him as "Candelita," which means *little torch,* or *little candle*—because his bright feathers would make them think of a pretty flame.

CHAPTER VII

MOTHER MAH-KAY
AND HER CUBS

MAH-KAY, the black bear, stood near a lake among the pines. Beside her sat Sooty and Cinnamon, two very little cubs.

Though the cubs were ten weeks old, they were having their first walk in the forest. They had never been out of their nursery den before. They had lived indoors ever since they were born, one day in late January. Their home was a hole dug in the side of a little hill under some fallen trees and a pile of broken branches. Mother Mah-kay had lined her den with dry leaves and twigs before the snow came. Later the snow fell and a big drift covered the pile of branches and filled the doorway. The only opening then was a small hole where Mah-kay's moist, warm breath came out. This showed as it rose in the frosty air like a little puff of steam.

When big Mah-kay's babies were born, they were only about eight inches long, and each weighed less than a pound. These small babies were nearly naked, for they had only a little fine hair on their pink bodies.

Mah-kay sat by a tree watching her cubs play.

They did not feel chilly, because their mother tucked them close to her and kept them covered with her long fur. She fed them plenty of good warm milk; and when they needed a bath, she washed them with her tongue.

With such good care, both babies grew and changed. In ten days they had soft grayish fur of their own, which became darker every day. Their eyes had been shut at first, but in six weeks these opened. There was not much for them to see in their dark den, but they began to toddle about. When they did that, Mother Mah-kay pulled her babies close to her with her paws and gave them little hugs to show them how proud she was that they could walk.

It was late March before the snow melted from the fallen trees above their home. That was the way the door to their den opened. The cubs were two months old when they had this chance to look out and see daylight for the first time in their lives, and to smell the fresh forest air. Soon Mah-kay walked toward the door. The cubs started to follow her, but their mother nudged them and pushed them back and sniffed in a way that made them understand that they must stay in their nursery. They were too young to go with her on her first spring trip to the lake.

Though Mah-kay had not eaten a thing for five months, she was not hungry. She had become very fat before going into her den, and this fat kept her healthy and strong during the winter. Indeed, Mah-kay did not think about finding something to eat even now. What she did think about was *water!* She had not had a drink for those five months either, and she was now so thirsty that she went down the snowy trail to the shore of the lake. Then she took a long drink. She lifted her head, said *"Woof!"* loudly, and drank again. Mah-kay drank so much water that her sides spread out, and her stomach was big and round. When she could not hold one more drop, she walked slowly back to her den and her babies.

After that, for two whole weeks Mah-kay left her cubs at home while she took a walk each day. At first she went just to drink, but in five or six days she felt hungry for spring food. So she dug up some roots to nibble.

At last, this sunny day in April, when the cubs were ten weeks old, Mother Mah-kay gave a new signal. She stood near the door of her den and grunted in a pleasant way. One cub got up and walked out to her. In a moment the other cub followed. Now that they were out in the sunlight, the colors of their fur coats could be seen. Though they had both had grayish fur while they were younger, one now had a black coat and the other had a brown one. So you may guess why we called these cubs Sooty and Cinnamon.

Mah-kay started down her trail and the little ones toddled after her, stumbling over sticks and slipping in the mud. Although their mother went very slowly, they could not keep up with her. When they felt tired, they began to whimper. Then Mah-kay came back to them, took them in her arms, and fed them warm milk. After they had rested, they were ready to go on a little farther.

When they reached the lake, Mah-kay took a drink,

Sooty liked to sit in the sun and play.

while the cubs looked at themselves in the water. They even tried to play with their queer reflections, and were much surprised when something wet splashed up and hit their black noses. With odd grunts they left the water and sat down on the shore. The quiet ground did not play splashy tricks on little cubs who were making their first visit in the big world of lakes and trees!

Soon Mother finished her long drink and joined them.

Instead of taking them straight back to the den, she led the way to a boggy place where skunk cabbages were just peeping through the damp, black soil. She dug some up and ate their roots, which were not so strongly flavored as they would be during late spring and summer.

After their first trip, the cubs followed their mother every day. For about a week they only watched or played while she dug up sprouting plants. Then they learned to nibble some of the tenderest roots. They learned, too, to take drinks of water, without getting splashed.

One day Mah-kay went fishing. She caught a large fish, throwing it out of the water with her paw. Both cubs liked its flaky, tender, white meat. They ate so much that little was left for their hungry mother. Now that they could eat and drink other things, they did not need so much milk as they had been drinking.

A few mornings later, Sooty and Cinnamon learned a new lesson. They were playing beside their mother when what seemed to them a very strange creature came through the woods. He walked noisily on two feet and made queer, shrill sounds with his mouth. When Mother Mah-kay heard those sounds, she signaled "Be quiet!" to her babies and then pushed them to the foot of a tree. That meant "Climb up!" and a couple of quick spanks meant "Hurry!" The cubs clambered up just as fast as they could and hung to a branch without moving. Mah-kay sat on the ground, so still that she looked like a dark rock. A man walked past a few yards away. He did not know that three bears watched him and listened to his happy whistling!

A few days later, Cinnamon, the brown cub, had an adventure. He wandered away from his sister and mother while they dozed beside some gray stones. First he chased a last year's leaf as it rolled and skipped along the ground in a gust of wind. Then he saw an early butterfly with brown wings bordered with yellow. He followed this up a hillside. When it flew too far to see, he spied a chipmunk and chased it until it disappeared. After that, he smelled something sweet and went still farther along the hill to hunt for it. When he could not find it, he sat up to look about him. He had wandered so far that he could not see his mother and Sooty. There were bushes all about him and he did not know where he was. He had lost his way.

A wise cub would have stopped, sniffed, and followed his own fresh trail down the hill. But the brown cub was too young to be wise. He climbed upon a flat stone, stretched his head up, and looked in all directions. Then he sat down and began to cry. He cried as loud as he could. He missed his mother and Sister Sooty very, very much.

Mother Mah-kay heard the noise in her sleep; and soon she was wide awake. She noticed that Cinnamon was gone, and she knew his thin, frightened voice. She gave Sooty a nudge that meant "Stay here!" and ran up the low hill. In three minutes, she crashed through the bushes and stopped beside her lost baby.

What do you think she did then? Did she cuddle him and tell him to stop crying? Did she try to tell him not to worry—that Mother would always take care of him?

No, she didn't! She gave the cub a spank that made him cry louder than ever. She hustled him off the flat stone and hurried him down the hillside. When he tried to stop, she spanked him again. After they got back to Sooty, she made her son sit still while she finished her nap. All the rest of that day the two cubs stayed very close to each other and very close to their mother.

Mah-kay did not slap her two furry children because she was angry. She loved them very dearly. She wanted them to learn how to take care of themselves. But until they knew how to find their way about, they must not ramble heedlessly into the great world of trees and bushes. If they were careless, she must punish them.

Both Sooty and her brown brother liked to sit in the sun and play with sticks. They liked, too, to take a pleasant woodland stroll and find good things for a picnic luncheon. They ate spicy red checkerberries and red partridge berries. These had formed the fall before but they were still plump and tasty in the spring. When the cubs came to an anthill, they usually stopped to eat some of these sour, stinging little creatures.[7]

Then there was a plant they were glad to find, though it had an even more burning taste than did the ants. They often dug up the wrinkled, turnip-shaped root of an Indian turnip (also called Jack-in-the-Pulpit), for they considered this a very good vegetable and seemed to enjoy its fiery juice.

But the very best feast those two cubs had was on the day their mother climbed an old hollow tree where bees had stored some honeycombs. Mah-kay tore away parts of the broken wood and it fell to the ground, honey and all. Mah-kay came down and ate some of it; but she left most of the honey for her twin cubs. It was the first time they had ever tasted anything so sweet.

Sooty and her brown brother never forgot that sticky treat. The memory of it stayed with them; and they made a game of climbing old hollow trees to see if honeybees had used them for hives.

[7] Ants have formic acid in them. An account of this is given in "Safety First among Animals," a chapter in *The Work of Scientists*.

CHAPTER VIII

HOO! HOOH!

"Hoo-oo, hoo! hoo! Hooo-hoo! hoo! Hoooh!"

These calls came from among the branches of a big birch tree that stood on a low hill. They began an hour after sunset, and they lasted until the moon came up. They were the calls in the love song that Bubo, the great horned owl, was singing to Opah, his mate.

Bubo found Opah on a snowy branch near the top of the tree. He sat beside her with spreading wings, but Opah half turned away. Then Bubo bowed, and hooted in what he meant to be a very pleasing voice. It did not seem pleasant to many creatures in the forest. Flying squirrels a mile away heard it, and sat very, very still until the last echo died away. How could they tell that the loud, hollow, strange sound was Bubo's love song instead of his hunting song?

Opah could tell, if the squirrels couldn't. After Bubo's first hoot, she turned toward him. Both owls fluffed their feathers, bobbed their heads, and side-stepped. Opah gave a faint, whispering hoot, and Bubo said *"Hoo!"* in a deep tone and rubbed his hooked beak

Bubo, the Great Horned Owl

gently against her face. Then the two owls bowed again and each rubbed the other's bill, hooting happily from time to time. Now and then Opah took short, sidling steps along the branch, as if she were going to leave Bubo. But she meant to do nothing of the sort. When Bubo did start to fly, Opah flapped her wings, too, and sailed away beside him.

Two days later the owls looked for a home. It was only the first week in March. Snow still covered the ground, and a recent storm had left the branches of the trees piled with white flakes. But Bubo and Opah did not mind cold weather. They did not even try to find a sheltered place. In fact, they chose an old deserted hawk's nest at the top of a tall maple that was exposed to every chilly wind that blew.

But it was a good strong nest, even if it wasn't new, and it saved the owls the trouble of building for themselves. Indeed, it was a better one than they could have put together. All Opah needed to do was to scoop out the snow and line the nest with some of her own warm feathers that were loose enough to pull out easily. Then she snuggled down in the hollow of her secondhand home, while Bubo perched on a pine tree near by. He waited there until it was dark enough for him to go hunting.

Snow was falling on Opah's fluffy back while she laid her first egg. It had a white, rather rough shell and it was a little more than two inches long. She sat on it all one night and day, but the second night she was so hungry that she flew away and caught a hare for supper.

Bubo did not cover the egg while she was gone; but he did perch near enough to see that nothing harmed it. Next day, Opah laid another egg; two days later, she laid a third one.

April came, and most of the snow melted, before Opah's three eggs hatched. The baby owls were blind and almost naked. When Opah left them to hunt, they lay on the feather bed in the nest and gave faint, whining peeps. If the weather was chilly, they shivered; but their mother took care not to leave them too long. She flew till she caught something for food and then hurried back to her nest.

When the nestlings were nine days old their eyes began to open. By that time brown feathers showed on their shoulders and backs; and they were strong enough to sit up when their mother left them. Their appetites had been good from the beginning and now they were eating a very great deal. Both Bubo and Opah worked hard to bring enough food to their hungry children. They liked any kind of meat their parents brought them—mice, rabbits, squirrels, and grouse often being on their bill of fare.

In the daytime, the owlets ate scraps that were left over from the night's supply. When they did this, Opah sat on the edge of the nest or perched beside it to give them room. Father Bubo sat in a tree near by, keeping in shadows as much as he could, for he did not like bright sunlight. He also felt sleepy during the day, for hunting and feeding the owlets kept him busy all night.

The owlets waiting for their supper.

There were some days, however, when Bubo could not sleep. This happened when blue jays bothered him. The jays spent much of their days flitting among trees, prying insects from cracks in the bark, and peeping into dark corners. If a blue jay saw Bubo, he would jump into the air and scream with excitement. He would flutter and hop about, calling for other jays to come to see what he had discovered. Other jays always came in a hurry and they screamed, too. They made so much noise that Bubo would fly to another tree, trying to find a quiet place. But the jays thought chasing a big owl was fun, so they rushed after him, yelling as they went. Finally, Bubo would shake his feathers with a savage gesture, sit close to a tree trunk, and snap his hooked beak angrily. The jays would keep out of Bubo's reach and scream till they grew tired of their bother-Bubo game, and went off to pry some more insects out of cracks.

Crows also chased and pestered Bubo by day. Crows and jays are rather close relatives and have many of the same habits. Some of these crows had had very narrow escapes from Bubo when he was hunting at their crow roost at night and they wanted to drive him out of their neighborhood. Sometimes a group of them would stay around the owl till evening—but then they hurried away. It would be careless of them to stay longer. In the daytime, they could get out of Bubo's way; but at night, he was much more alert than even the cleverest crow.

When the owlets were a month old, they were almost as big as hens, and were covered with fluffy feathers. They hopped about on the nest and spread their wings for exercise. As they grew, they needed more and more food and their parents certainly had to do a lot of hunting. Bubo was quite pleased when he caught a muskrat for them in the swamp near the lake.

The next evening Bubo went back to the lake and got a quite different supper for the owlets. No jays had bothered him that day, and he was feeling cheerful. It seemed a good time to go fishing. Swooping past the muddy end of the lake, he saw a fish in water so shallow that part of its back stuck above the surface.

Without a sound, Bubo pounced, closed his talons, and picked up the fish without even wetting his leg feathers. Then he hurried away to the nestlings. This was the first fish they had ever eaten and they seemed to think pike meat very good—though they swallowed it in such big gulps that they did not spend much time tasting it.

Of course, the owlets could not eat *everything* their father and mother brought them. The big head of the pike was too tough to swallow. It lay in the nest all day; then Opah picked it up in her beak, flew off with it, and dropped it. She carried away big rabbit bones and other things they couldn't eat, for she was careful to keep their home tidy for the nestlings.

One night, when Bubo came to the nest, his feathers had a strange, strong odor. It made the owlets blink their eyes and sneeze. Bubo did not seem to mind it much, though he did give his queer-smelling feathers some attention. He perched on a treetop near the nest, to smooth and fluff and air them carefully.

Bubo went hunting.

Mother Opah guessed what had happened—can you? Bubo had called the loud *"Hoo-hoo-hooh!"* as he usually did before hunting. Just then something moved near the shore of the lake, something black and furry, with white stripes and a big, bushy tail. It was a skunk, hunting for beetles. Bubo knew what skunks are like before he pounced. He had met them before, so he was not one bit surprised at the odor that suddenly came around him like a cloud. A deer near by coughed, gasped, and galloped away; a fox wrinkled his long nose and hurried through the bushes. But Bubo calmly carried his prey to the bare branch of a dead tree and ate the best of it for supper before he caught a small rabbit to take to his nestlings.

One June evening, as the sun set, Bubo flew from his pine tree and perched on one edge of the nest. Opah hopped to the other side. Soon both old owls began to push and coax their three children. They wanted the youngsters to leave the nest, but the owlets were too timid to go. They whined, dodged, and snapped their beaks, and then they sat down and begged for food.

What happened later no one knows, for the night was very dark. But when morning came the big nest was empty. One owlet was perched on a leafy birch limb. Another sat in Bubo's pine. The third was settled beside Opah in a white-cedar tree. There they dozed and blinked until sunset. In the pleasant, dim evening light, they opened their yellow eyes wide, snapped their beaks, bobbed their heads, and watched Bubo and Opah make ready for their night's hunting. The old owls perched for a while on dead trees where there were no leaves to prevent them from seeing moving things.

Did the owlets follow them? Not then. They still were too young, clumsy, and untrained. They must spend several weeks flying, listening, and learning before they, too, could perch on treetops, ready to go hunting for themselves.

CHAPTER IX

CHIPPY AND KAN

A Chipmunk and His Burrow

On a bright spring afternoon, the sun warmed a corner in the forest. A chipmunk in his burrow underground felt the pleasant heat. He twisted and yawned until he was really awake. Then he poked his sharp nose out of doors, blinking in the sunlight. Soon he ran to a log and sat upon it while he cleaned his fur. It was dusty after his winter-long sleep in the dark burrow.

Chippy's fur was brown, black, and gray on the back, with a dark stripe down the middle. On each of his sides were two more dark stripes, with a creamy-white band between them. His chest and underside were white. Chippy spent a long time combing the dust from his soft, white underfur.

When he stopped combing and cleaning, Chippy scampered along the log. He paused at a broken branch, sat up straight, and began to sing. *"Chuck, chuck, chuck-a-chuck!"* he called, over and over again. Then his voice became low and soft. It made a pretty, warbling sound, like the song of a bird.

76

Chippy's music roused other chipmunks who also had left their burrows. Some of them only sat up and stretched, still looking very sleepy while they listened. Others raised their heads and sang. They called, *"Chuck, chuck!"* or *"Chir, chirr, chirrr!"* and then gave the sweet warble. There was one chipmunk who was too young to warble. The best he could do was to call *"Chip, chip, chip!"* in a thin, squeaky voice.

After singing, Chippy felt thirsty. First he looked up into the air and then along the ground. There was no hawk sailing above him and no hungry weasel or mink moving near the log. So Chippy ran safely to a pool made by melting snow. There he crouched on all four feet and took a long sip. He had to take three of those sips to get all the water he wanted.

Drinking made Chippy hungry. He did not find any good chipmunk food lying about among the damp leaves on the ground or dangling from branches that spring day. But that did not trouble Chippy. All he had to do was to scamper back to his burrow. There he had a round room stored with acorns, maple seeds, and dry berries. He nibbled two acorns and several dry black currants before he went to bed.

After his first outing, Chippy left his burrow every warm day. Sometimes, he hopped to a stump and sang; often, he played with his neighbor chipmunks. They had fine games of tag among the logs, bushes, and roots. They even climbed mountain-ash shrubs and the bushy mountain maples, chasing one another from branch to branch.

*Chippy liked acorns and maple seeds: 1—leaves and acorns
of the bur oak, which is also called "mossy-cup" oak.
2—leaves and seeds of the sugar maple, or rock maple.*

One morning, after going out for his drink, Chippy would not play. He had work to do. His home was dry and comfortable, but it needed a new doorway or two. Chippy hurried back into his tunnel and began to dig.

He dug beneath a fallen pine tree. When he dug all the way to the surface, he came out among the tangled pine roots. That was a good place for a door, since the roots, like a fine fence, would keep unwelcome creatures from flying or running into Chippy's home.

Chippy was so well pleased that he went back and began to dig again. This time, he came out under a red raspberry bush. This was still better! The bramble would be a spiny hedge to stop owls or hawks, while the berries were good to eat when they turned red.

Chippy now had three doors—one more than he really needed. He carried dirt from the pile at the entrance of his last tunnel and poured it into the old tunnel. He got rid of most of the pile that way, but not all. Chippy took the rest away in his cheek pouches and scattered it here and there. Last of all, he covered the filled door with leaves, sticks, and bits of dry moss. Not even a prowling weasel could tell that there once had been a hole under that rubbish.

So much digging, filling, and carrying took a long time. One week went by and then another before Chippy's work was done. When the old door was hidden and the new ones were put in tidy shape, he took a holiday. He slept late, and ate a bigger breakfast than usual—acorns from his pantry, and some fresh plant shoots that grew out of doors. Then he sat on the pine log to comb his fur. He sang a few *chuck-a-chucks,* but did not warble once.

Though Chippy was rather tired, he was as alert as ever. His black eyes watched the sky, the trees, and the ground. He saw Bomby, the waxwing, perched on a branch, while two chickadees hunted insects in a maple tree. He heard Walloon "laugh" far out on the lake, and he watched a grouse poking among the dead leaves. Since none of these neighbors ever bothered him, he went on combing his fur.

Soon, a motion of wings overhead caused Chippy to take a careful look toward the sky. What he saw that time made him jump from the log, scamper to the raspberry bushes, and dodge into his new door. While he ran, a bluish-gray hawk swooped down, very, very fast. It stretched out its feet, with their long, sharp, curved claws—but just then Chippy was rushing out of sight in his hallway underground. The hawk spread its wings and flapped quickly away to keep from touching the prickly raspberry bushes.

Chippy heard the hawk's wings go *zoom!* and he peeped out as the big bird flew away. Soon he bobbed out of his burrow again, but he did not go far from the door for some time. For all he knew, that swift hawk might come back. If it did, Chippy would be close to his door under the spiny raspberry hedge.

KAN, THE FLYING SQUIRREL

When Chippy and his friends sang very loudly, they often wakened Kan, the flying squirrel, and his brother. They both liked to sleep during the day. If the chipmunks wakened them, they generally yawned, snuggled closer together, and then dozed again. Sometimes one of them peeped out of his door to see what forest dweller was making so much noise.

The flying squirrel never peeped long. Sunlight made him blink his eyes, and the brightness did not tempt him to come out among the trees. Kan or Brother would take one look and then curl down again in the comfortable, dark, warm home.

That home was a hole in a dead maple tree. Two

The chipmunks chattered so loudly that they woke Kan.

woodpeckers had dug it to hold their eggs. When the woodpecker family grew up and flew away, a little brown bat moved in. After a while, however, the bat went somewhere else, and Kan found the empty woodpecker hole. He and his brother played near it one night. When morning came, they slipped inside. It was so warm and cozy that they decided to live in it. They never thought that the woodpecker and his mate might want the hole when spring would come again.

Their new home was good, but it was not perfect. Kan scraped out some hard chips which the woodpeckers had left. His brother brought pieces of bark from a cedar tree. Then he and Kan worked together, tearing the bark into strips so thin and slender that they looked almost like hair. These fine strips kept the two squirrels from becoming chilly in even the coldest weather.

Now that it was spring, Kan and his brother did not need quite so much bedding. Their own furry coats were enough to keep them warm while they stayed at home in the daytime.

As the sun set, the chipmunks stopped playing and hurried to their homes. Crows, who had flown about and called *"Caw, Caw,"* stopped talking and went to sleep in a pine tree. A red squirrel who had scolded the crows curled up in his nest near the top of a big birch.

While these day-creatures were getting drowsy, Kan became wide awake. He yawned, stretched, and nipped his brother's ear for fun. Then he whisked through his round door and scampered out to a bare branch. When

Kan sat on a branch while his brother sailed through the air.

his brother came out, the two ran a race round and round the trunk of the old maple tree.

Next, Kan climbed a pine tree. He ran up it just like any other squirrel. But when he got to a high branch, he jumped and sailed to a lower branch on another tree, almost forty feet away. Sometimes he would swoop even farther before landing on the ground. When he jumped from a high place and started to sail, he spread his legs widely. This stretched the folds of skin between them until his body looked like a squarish kite with a long, fluffy tail. The back of the living "kite" was covered by soft brown fur, with blackish lines along the sides. Its under parts were white, because of the white fur that covered Kan's throat and the lower part of his body.

After climbing, jumping, and sailing so much, Kan began to feel hungry. He liked the small rich seeds that grow in spruce cones. He liked nuts. He liked insects of certain kinds when he could find them. But that night he ran up a tree and nibbled some leaf buds from the tips of twigs. Then he remembered where there was a bush with red berries. The berries were dry, but they still tasted good. He soared to the ground, climbed into the bush, and was soon nibbling the dry fruit as fast as he had been eating buds.

Kan's brother, too, was busy eating when the flying squirrels both heard an owl call. They did not run and hide. They did not soar down to the ground. They just stopped eating and sat perfectly still until the big, hungry bird flew away. Then they finished their meal before climbing to treetops and sailing to low branches or to the ground.

After one climb, Kan paused. The sky was turning blue-gray, which meant that morning was near. With a swoop, he sailed to the dead maple where Brother already was perched. The two little animals smoothed their soft fur and then slipped into their nest. They were not really tired, of course, but what flying squirrel wants to play in the bright, clear sunshine? They would leave all that sort of thing to the chipmunks and other day-creatures.

Mother Walloon and her two eggs.

CHAPTER X

BIRDS OF A FOREST LAKE

"*Ha-ha-ha-ha-ha!*" sang Imber Diver as he swam across the lake at sunrise. He was happy that May morning when he gave his call which sounded somewhat like a howling laugh. His voice seemed strange to a man in a tent in the woods near the shore of the lake. But Imber was a loon, and of course many things a loon does seem strange to a man.

Walloon did not think there was anything queer about Imber's screaming chuckle. Since Walloon was Imber's mate, she naturally was used to his voice and his ways. She listened with pleasure after the *ha-ha* call until she heard Imber change his tune and make a soft, almost cooing sound. She knew he was asking her to come to play a morning game with him, so she swam to meet him.

To begin with, Imber and Walloon raced across the lake. They half spread their short wings, worked their legs and webbed feet like paddles, and lifted their big black-and-white bodies almost out of the water.

Off they went, flapping and splashing until they had raced far enough. Then they stopped, folded their wings, and dived. They swam under water for about half a minute before they came back to the surface again, quite a long way from the place where they went down. They took deep breaths, "laughed" together, and swam in curves and zigzags, as if they were very happy.

The loons swam on a lake that lay among green forests.

After all this exercise, the two loons were so hungry that they paddled to their favorite fishing place. Here, Walloon and Imber floated quietly until they saw some young pikes. Then they dived and swam toward the fish very swiftly. Imber missed his aim by an inch, but Walloon caught a fine pike crosswise in her beak. With a quick toss of her head, she brought the fish's head into her throat, stretched her neck, and swallowed. The fish seemed to work its own way down her long, slender throat.

The two loons took a second dive and that time Imber caught a fish. But one young pike was not enough for a meal, so they tried to find more. The rest of the fish, however, had hurried away; and the loons skimmed off to some shallows, where they caught several spotted frogs. They found some leeches, too, that tasted good to them. Then they finished their breakfast by eating a few water plants which they pulled up by the roots.

Walloon now decided to fly, but she could not merely sail away. Her heavy body weighed ten pounds and her wings were not long like those of a gull. She swung around, so that she faced the breeze. If she had not done that, she might have fallen back as soon as she tried to leave the water. Even facing the wind, she half ran, half flew for a long way, beating the water with her wings before she "took off."

As Walloon flapped into the air, Imber managed to get started, too. In a few minutes, both loons were flying above the forest that surrounded their little lake. They flew with their heads and necks stretched forward, and their wings working very rapidly. Sometimes they went in straight lines; at other times they sailed in big circles. Every minute or two, they opened their beaks and gave calls that sounded like *"Ah-o-ooh! Ah-o-ooh!"* and ended with two or three *ha-has*.

When they wanted to alight, the loons used almost as much space as they did when they started flying, for their wings were not big enough to stop the movement of their bodies quickly. They had to circle lower and lower, until they knew they could stand the shock of sliding into the water. Then they settled with a great splash which sent spray flying. Even then, they rushed a long way across the water before they finally stopped.

Night came after a day of play and laughter, but the loons did not go ashore. Instead, they swam far from land and went to sleep, side by side, floating upon the water. Long before sunrise, Imber awoke, rousing Walloon with his *"Ah-o-oooh!"* call. He thought it was time to get ready for a breakfast of frogs, leeches, fish, and a few bites of plants.

After they had eaten their breakfast, Imber started to fly; but Walloon did not go with him. Instead, she made a few cooing sounds and swam to a low, rocky point that jutted out from the forest. There she stopped and scrambled out of the water, stumbling rather awkwardly on the damp, stony ground.

A few lurches brought her to a flat place, hidden by bushes and rocks. She had discovered this retreat three years before when she and Imber first came to this lake in the deep forest. She had made her nest there each year since she found it; and she would return to it at nesting time as long as she lived—unless, of course, something happened to spoil it. Neither she nor Imber cared to move to a different home after settling in such a safe and secret spot.

The high water in the lake earlier in the spring had washed across the little home lot and carried away most of last year's nest. For the floor of her new nest, Walloon chose a place where moss an inch deep covered both the damp soil and the small, round stones. She gathered some twigs and pulled up moss which she piled in a broad rim around the mossy center. Her building, when it was finished, was almost two feet across. The mossy, hollow place in the middle was about sixteen inches wide and three inches deep.

After all this work was done, Walloon slipped away to find Imber and go for a swim. Soon after she met her mate, the two loons saw Mer Ganser and his flock. These were ducks who also could dive and catch fish under water. Their upper beaks had saw-tooth edges which kept the fish from wriggling away. They had crests of thin, rather stiff feathers. The breast feathers of the mother birds were white, while the male ducks had brownish-red feathers which showed why they were called "red-breasted" mergansers.

When Mer Ganser and his companions saw Walloon and Imber Diver coming, they skimmed away rather swiftly. They seemed to think that the loons would rather have that part of the lake to themselves. After the ducks had gone, Imber and Walloon began to dive and play. Sometimes they swam a long way under water, sinking and rising in a game that seemed a bit like hide-and-seek. At other times they swam close to the surface, with only their beaks in the air. They looked like black sticks drifting across the lake—until one of the loons came to the surface and called *"O-o-ooh!"* or *"Ha-ha-ha!"*

The next morning, after eating and playing for a little while, Walloon hurried away to her nest. There she snuggled down on the basin of moss, keeping very,

Mer Ganser, the duck, always swam away
when the loons came to his part of the lake.

very quiet. When she finally got up, a big, olive-brown egg with brown spots lay upon the moss. Walloon looked at the egg several times, and did not leave it until Father Imber came ashore. He was just as awkward as Walloon when he stepped on land. He bent forward and stumbled along, using his wings to help him walk. But he was willing to leave the lake long enough to sit on the nest while his mate went fishing.

Walloon covered the egg all night, while Imber floated and slept on the water, only a few rods away. During the next forenoon Imber waited near by, taking a few lonely dives and poking among odd corners made by rocks and fallen trees. At last, a faint sound brought him back. He stumbled in a hopping sort of way over the stones to the nest and stood beside Walloon for a few minutes before she moved to one side and started for the water.

Imber looked down. Two eggs, instead of just one, lay in the nest—all that Walloon would lay. Her mate moved the second egg with his beak, slipped over them carefully, and covered them with his feathers. He was ready to do his share of sitting during the four weeks that must pass before those eggs would hatch into sturdy youngsters covered with stiff, black down.

What would the baby loons do when they hatched? They would not waste their time on land. They would go into the lake and stay there with their parents. For water would be their home both night and day.

Water, too, would be their home winter as well as summer; though of course they could not spend the coldest months in a frozen lake. Instead, the old loons and the young, who would be full grown before that time, would fly to the salt water of the Atlantic Ocean, where there was no icy crust even in January. And there in the sea the happy Divers would play and fish and laugh!

CHAPTER XI

THA, THE MARTEN

THE April sun shone on the forest. It changed the last, icy snowdrifts to water that sank in the sticky mud. It started the sap flowing in birches and poplars. It warmed Bubo's owlets so they did not shiver, even when their mother left them and perched near the nest.

The sunshine also brought comfort to Tha, the marten, when he crept out of his den in the hollow of an old white-pine tree. The den once belonged to two big woodpeckers, but they moved out when Tha moved in. It was easy enough for them to find another old tree in which they could dig a hollow home; and a marten is not the kind of neighbor woodpeckers enjoy.

Why? Well, there are several reasons. For one thing, martens like to eat eggs for breakfast; and those woodpeckers had another use for their eggs!

But Tha was not looking for breakfast or dinner when he left his den that April day. He was not especially hungry. He was not a fat winter-sleeper like Mah-kay, the black bear; and even in cold weather he had left his den, whenever he was hungry enough to go hunting.

What he wanted just then was warm sunshine—plenty of warm sunshine.

For a while, Tha stood on a broken branch of his old pine tree, sunning his fur. This was mostly yellowish brown, though his legs were blackish and his throat and chest were orange. His pale claws looked white when he put them against the dark weather-worn wood.

After standing there for a few minutes, blinking in the bright light, Tha suddenly remembered something. Why not take his sun bath high, high up in his favorite nest?

That nest was in the top of a dead maple that stood on a rocky knoll some distance away. But Tha did not climb down the old pine trunk and run over the ground to reach the maple. Instead, he climbed to a long branch on the other side of his white pine and followed it until he could jump to a hemlock not far away. He walked along one of its branches and jumped again, catching hold of twigs to steady himself and swinging on them as fearlessly as a squirrel.

In this way, climbing and leaping, Tha followed a branch trail leading from hemlock to spruce, from spruce to jack pine, and so on until he reached a branch of the dead maple. He ran along the branch to the trunk, climbed to the top very quickly, and stopped at a big, deserted nest.

Hawks had built the nest the year before. After they were through with it, Tha had discovered that it was a good place for a nap in the sun. It seemed just as

Tha stood on a broken branch.

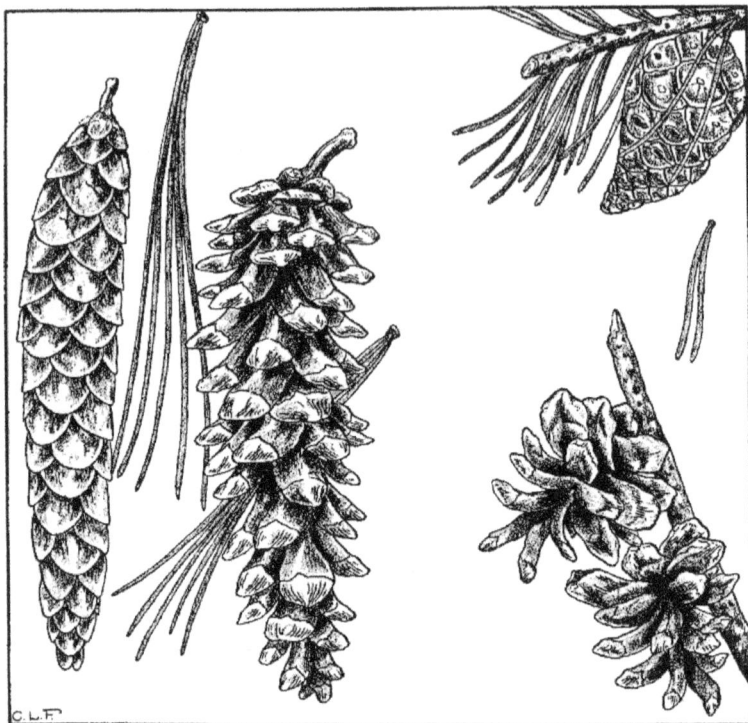

White pines and jack pines grew in Tha's forest.

This picture shows open and closed cones of white pine (left) and jack pine (right) and clusters of leaves, or "needles." The white pine has five needles in each bundle and the jack pine has two.

comfortable that spring day as it had in the fall. Tha yawned, cuddled down, and shut his black, shiny eyes.

The marten lay in the nest until late afternoon. He was so quiet that crows, flapping overhead, did not notice him. A pair of ravens soared past, hoarsely calling "*Kurr-karr*"; but they seemed to be seeking a nest of their own, not one left by last year's hawks. Blue jays whined and chattered below, but did not happen to go to the top of the maple. Tha was glad of that. When blue jays saw him, they always dashed about him, making such a racket that he hurried back to his den to be rid of them.

Before sunset, Tha left the nest. He moved very quickly, looking from side to side and smelling with his long, keen nose. If there was anything interesting in that part of the forest, Tha would see it, smell it, and find out what it was. If it was good to eat, he probably would try to find it.

To be sure, there were the three hungry youngsters of Bubo, the great horned owl, near by. They had toddled to the edge of the nest and peeped over. Their big, yellow eyes stared at Tha as he went down the trunk of the maple. The marten, however, did not stop to stare back. He knew better than to hunt horned owls even when they were babies. Their parents were both on guard and Tha did not care to meet them.

Instead of traveling over a branch-route this evening, Tha loped along the ground. He moved gracefully, even though his legs were so short that his body almost touched the ground. He arched his back, lifted his bushy tail, and took care to keep out of the soft mud. He jumped across small pools of water and hurried around big ones.

Tha did not like to get water on his fur or wet his feet. On a rainy day, he would stay in his den rather than get soaked. A sun bath was a joy—but what marten would care to take a water bath?

On one slope, Tha stopped to sniff at some tracks whose toeprints showed plainly. They were made by

Vison, the mink, who was a relative of Tha. (They both belong to the Weasel Family.) Vison's tracks led to the shallow edge of a lake where he had gone to catch a fish or a frog for his supper.

Supper? Why, yes—Tha was hungry, too. What should he have? He would like a fish or a frog; but he certainly was not going to get his fur wet hunting for them! Well, never mind, there were many other things that Tha could eat. He relished any kind of meat he could catch, whether it walked on two legs like a grouse, on four legs like a mouse, or on six legs like an insect.

Tha enjoyed fruit, too; and he paused when he came to some shrubby, little mountain-ash trees. He had often feasted, during the fall, on the bright orange-red berries that grew on these trees. Many clusters had stayed on the trees after the snow came, and these had been a most important winter food for him. A few bunches of berries still dangled from the branches. They were now hard and dry, instead of plump and soft as they had been in the fall. But Tha climbed up and ate them gladly, pulling them to his mouth with his front paws.

Just as Tha finished his berries, something rustled in the dead leaves that covered the ground. With a jump, Tha landed on it, his paws digging through the leaves. *Nip!* went his teeth, catching the mouse that had been making faint rustling sounds as he moved. Tha ate the mouse in three bites and thought it very, very good.

A few berries and one mouse were not enough for a real meal, though; and Tha started for his hidden pantry. He had a chunk of rabbit meat put away under

Tha did most of his hunting in the thick woods.

some rubbish at the side of an old log. For Tha was not wasteful. When he caught more meat than he needed, he buried what was left under sticks and fallen leaves. He would come back to it the next day, or the next, when hunting was not so good.

Tha did not go all the way to his pantry that April evening, however. He found all he wanted before he got there. Along the trail, Tha came to a rock where two forest rangers had stopped to cook their dinner that noon. They had been fishing and had caught one more fish than they needed. This they had left beside the rock, as a gift to some hungry forest creature. So Tha was lucky, after all. His supper was just as good as that of Cousin Vison, the mink—and he didn't even have to wet his paws to get it!

After finishing his supper, Tha cleaned his whiskers and started back toward his den. Near the maple, he met his mate. He had not seen her since early March, when they spent a day and a night together at her home in a hollow, dead birch tree. When morning came, Tha left her—and his mate did not urge him to stay. Marten mates do not spend much time together. Their habits are quite different from those of bears, beavers, and many other furry animals.

Mrs. Tha was not even glad to meet her mate that April evening. Indeed, she stopped in the middle of a leap, bared her sharp teeth, and snarled.

But she did not hurt Tha's feelings. He didn't mind in the least. He did not care about being sociable, either. He turned aside, jumped over some tangled roots, and ran under some bushes to the foot of his own tree. He climbed quickly up its rough, dark bark and darted into the mouth of his den.

The air had grown chilly, so Tha curled up tightly and covered his nose with his tail. For half an hour he kept his eyes open, watching the yellow glow of sunset as it faded from the sky. As the first star twinkled, he yawned deeply. By the time night settled down and Bubo started hunting, Tha was sound asleep at the bottom of his den in the big, old pine.

CHAPTER XII

VEERY

THE sun was just setting one June evening and the light was fading among the quiet trees. Suddenly a loud call broke the twilight silence. It was a startling sound, sharp and harsh. Veery was speaking.

Veery, the Wilson thrush, had flown to a branch on a chokecherry tree. There were taller trees on all sides, but Veery did not care to go very high. He turned his head after his first call and spoke again. This time his voice sounded as if it came from a different place, but Veery was still on the same branch.

A moment later, music filled the air, a rich, mellow whistle that seemed to whirl in circles—full and loud at first and then soft as a whisper. Veery was singing.

While Veery was singing, his mate was on her nest keeping four eggs warm. The eggs were greenish-blue, much like those of a robin only smaller. It was not at all strange that Mrs. Veery's eggs should resemble those of Mrs. American Robin, for both of these birds belong to the Thrush Family.

Father Veery perched on the branch of a chokecherry tree.

Mrs. Veery's own colors, however, were quite different from those of Cousin Robin. She did not have a reddish breast. Her underfeathers were white, with some pale brown streaks and spots on the upper part of her breast. Her back was tawny brown.

The nest of the tawny thrush was not like Cousin Robin's nest. Its walls were not made of mud. They were built with dry grass, narrow strips of birch bark, and torn bits of leaves, with soft, dry moss for a lining. There were eight tiny "timbers" in the foundation. One timber was a piece of dry goldenrod stem nine inches long. The others were slender stems of dry sumac leaves.

Many tawny thrushes build their nests on the ground, but this Mrs. Veery and her mate had made a platform for their nest on the lowest branches of a young spruce tree. They brought nearly fifty dry, brown oak leaves for this platform.

Veery sat on the eggs when his mate wished to go away from the nest, but he did not talk or sing then. Like most birds, these thrushes considered their nest to be their own secret. Every time Veery came near it, he was very cautious. He flew to an oak branch and paused there to look and listen.

Next he reached a sumac bush and stopped there while he looked and listened again. His third perch was the branch of a low birch. Then he took a short, quick turn and arrived at the nest.

It was the twenty-eighth of June when those thrushes began to keep their four eggs warm, and the eggs took about twelve days to hatch. During all this time the birds were silent while they were on or near the nest.

But once, after the eggs had hatched and the baby birds were a few days old, both Father and Mother Veery made a racket. That was the day when Chickaree, the red squirrel, found out their secret by running up the little spruce tree and seeing the nest.

Father Veery sat on a near-by sumac branch and yelled "Here! *Here!* HERE! HERE!" Mother Veery came near the other side of the nest and called "Dear! *Dear!* DEAR DEAR!"

All the birds in that edge of the woods heard the thrushes and knew that they were begging for help. First, a purple finch fluttered between the birch branches and began to scold the squirrel. Next, a flicker dashed down and yelped at it. Then several warblers flew back and forth, chattering and jabbering in protest. A robin came and started to shout, but by that time there was no red squirrel to scold. Where was Chickaree? Oh, he had jumped to the ground and scampered out of sight among the bushes.

The excitement was all over. Father Veery stood on the leafy platform and watched the nest. Mother Veery went off to find some caterpillars to feed the young birds. When she came back, Father took his turn at hunting. Those Veery babies were growing so fast that they needed a great deal of food.

They grew so fast, indeed, that by the time they were nine days old, two of them filled the nest. There was no room for the other two inside that home—they

The young Veeries left their porch and
fluttered to another tree.

were crowded out. They did not object, however; for they were just as happy and comfortable on the leafy platform outside the nest. The dry oak leaves served as a very good porch for them. They waited there while their father and mother brought them insects to eat.

The next day (which was July the twentieth) none of the young birds was in the nest. They had all even left their porch. They were using their wings for the first time. The youngsters fluttered from low branches to the ground in awkward, heavy flops of ten or twelve feet.

It was well for them to practice flying, for they would need to use their wings for a long, long journey. Some day in September the Veeries would be starting south; and perhaps they would go as far as Brazil to spend the winter. On the way, they would stop for frequent picnic luncheons. They would feast on wild fruit, and bitter chokecherries would be one of their favorite treats.

But they would come back to northern woods in the spring. And there at dawn of day and evening dusk, a sweet mellow whistle would whirl through the air— full and rich and loud at first and then soft as a whisper. Veery would be singing again!

CHAPTER XIII

BROWN-WING OF THE FOREST

TELEA brown-wing sat on an old log near an open place in the forest. Sunshine twinkled between the green leaves above and fell upon her wings. They were big, light, buff-brown wings with pink and dark stripes near their margins; and each had a glassy-clear spot near the middle. The clear spots on the hind wings were edged with colors that made them look a bit like the pretty "eyespots" on peacocks' tail feathers. The wings were still limp, but the sun was making them stiff and strong. They would be ready to use when night came, and Telea did not care to fly in the daytime.

Less than three hours had passed since Telea crawled out of a cocoon, much as if she were hatching. She wasn't really hatching, of course. She had done that the summer before. That was when she came from a flat, creamy-white egg with a brown band, on a leaf of a red-oak tree.

That egg was just one among more than two hundred eggs that Telea's mother laid. While she was laying them, she waved her wings slowly to and fro and walked from one leaf to another with her six jointed legs.

Telea Brown-wing sat on an old log.

She fastened small bunches of eggs to the leaves with a kind of mucilage that she made in her body.

After Telea's mother had laid all her eggs, she rested a while and then flew away. She never came back to brood her eggs. She did not have a warm body like a bird's, and the sun gave them all the heat they needed. Telea's mother never came back to take care of her babies after they hatched, either; but they did not miss her. She had left her eggs right where her young children could find plenty of their favorite food without any further help from her.

When Telea hatched, she was not a brown moth, like her mother. She was a tiny, greenish-yellow caterpillar, with yellow spots and a brick-red head. After she nibbled her way out of the eggshell, she found herself on a flat leaf-world that stretched out on all sides of her. But Telea did not lose her way. She crawled to the edge of the leaf and began to eat.

Near her were other caterpillars, Telea's own brothers and sisters. They also crawled to the edge of the leaf and began to bite it with their tiny black jaws. One of them got in Telea's way. When they met, both caterpillars wriggled about and started to nibble in opposite directions.

Day after day, from morning to night, Telea ate leaves. When one leaf was gone, she crawled to another. Her brothers and sisters crawled, too. Luckily for them, the oak tree was big and had thousands of leaves. Had it been a young sapling, the caterpillars might have eaten until its twigs were bare!

Even on the big tree, the caterpillars might have eaten too many leaves for the good of the tree, if it had not been for birds who came there to hunt. These birds ate some of the caterpillars and carried some to babies in their nests. Thus, the tree had enough leaves for its own needs—and plenty to spare for the caterpillars that were left.

Telea, herself, did not get caught. Once she escaped only because she kept very still, for a very long time. A hungry bird who was hunting caterpillars didn't notice that her green body was not really just a part of a leaf!

Some of Telea's food gave her energy for work, such as eating and crawling. But most of her food was used for growth. Indeed, she had been eating only six or seven days when her body became much too large for her skin. She felt squeezed and uncomfortable. What could she do about it?

What Telea did was to hump up her back behind her head and wriggle until her tight skin split. Then she crept out of her old skin and left it on the leaf, like a worn-out dress that had been thrown away. A new loose skin had formed over her body under the old tight one. So now she was comfortable again in a skin that could stretch while she ate and grew. About a week later, this second skin became so snug that Telea shed it, too. In this way, she shed her skin, or "molted," four times while she was growing up. After the last skin-change, she grew to be a beautiful, plump caterpillar almost three inches long. Her skin was a bright, clear green with golden yellow and orange spots. Her eyes glowed like opals when the sun shone on them.

Telea stopped in a paper-birch tree,
near a cocoon spun by one of her brothers.

One day, after she had been eating for about seven weeks, Telea lost her appetite for oak leaves. Instead of feasting, she went for a little journey. She crawled from a leaf to a twig and then to the trunk of the oak tree. She hurried headfirst down the trunk to the ground, and then rushed over to an elm tree which she started to climb. But after going part way up the trunk, she stopped, turned, and crawled back to the ground. She wandered about for a few minutes, meeting some ants that were in the way. They nipped her as she passed, but Telea walked right over these small, black insects.

Soon Telea came to a paper-birch sapling and climbed that in a hurry. She stopped near something that looked like a pale tan, oval ball wrapped in leaves. Though Telea did not know it, the ball was a cocoon, spun just the day before by one of her own brothers.

Now that her journey was over, Telea rested for some time on her birch twig. If she had happened to hatch on a birch leaf seven weeks before, she would have eaten birch leaves with relish. But she did not even taste one now. She had already swallowed the last bit of food she wanted.

Soon Telea went to work on her own cocoon. She curled up between two leaves and began to spin threads of silk. This silk was formed in two silk glands inside Telea's body. While in the glands, the silk was a sticky liquid. Telea squeezed it out through a tube that had an opening in her lower lip. As soon as the liquid silk touched the air, it stiffened into a thread.

Telea was one of the "giant silkworms," and the

silk that she made was very good indeed. As a matter of fact, people (if they wished to do so) could use silk fibers like Telea's to make silk cloth, as they use the silk of the Cynthia caterpillar, another kind of "giant silkworm" that lives in Asia. As you may know, pongee cloth is woven from silk spun by these Asiatic "giant silkworms"; but most silk cloth is woven from fibers spun by "mulberry silkworms," who are not "giants." [8]

While Telea was working, she moved her head back and forth to swing her silk fiber where it should go to make her oval cocoon, or "sleeping bag." There were so many loops in her cocoon that she had to move her head to and fro more than two hundred thousand times to make them all! When it was finished, it was fastened tightly to the leaves, while several loose threads of silk held it to the birch twig.

Inside the cocoon, Telea shed her skin again. When she wriggled out of this skin, she was no longer a caterpillar. She had lost her bright green color and her golden spots. She had no creeping-legs, or "pro-legs." Her head, with its chewing jaws, was gone. She had become a "pupa" with a shiny brown, shell-like case within which still more changes were taking place.

Pressed tightly against the inside of this pupa case were the forms of four wing pads, two featherlike feelers, and six legs. Telea could not move her wing pads, her feelers or her legs. She could only jerk or wiggle the joints near the pointed end of the pupa. She didn't even

[8] More is told about these and other little silkmakers in "Silk," a chapter in *Science at Home.*

do that very much. During most of the time for months she lay as still as if she were sound asleep.

Fall came and the birch tree shed its leaves. The cocoons swung for a while on loose threads of silk. Then one breezy day they fell to the ground, too, and in time were covered with snow.

At last, spring followed a long winter. New leaves grew on the trees. Chickadees built nests in holes. Seto, the redstart, came from his winter home in South America. But Telea still remained a pupa. Except for a wriggle now and then, she seemed as sound asleep as ever.

One June afternoon, she wriggled much harder than she had done before and the brown shell of her pupa split open. Telea squirted some liquid on one end of the cocoon, causing the silk fibers there to become soft and weak. She pushed against this moist end and it opened like a door just big enough to let her squeeze through. When she was outside, she made her way to a fallen birch branch and hung there upside down, clinging to the branch with her legs.

Telea was now a moth—but what a queer thing she seemed at first! Her downy body was damp and her wings, which were only small flaps, hung in wrinkles. She pumped some clear, colorless liquid from her body into the veins in her wings. While she was doing this, the wings expanded until they were full-sized. The down on her body was now dry and fluffy. After a while, she walked along the branch until she came to a log. There she would sit until her wings became stiff and strong.

While Telea waited, the sun set and the dusk of early evening settled over the forest. Mice scampered among the leaves. Tha, the marten, awoke and climbed down from his hole in the hollow pine. Bubo, the owl, called *"Hoo-hoo-hooosk!"* and then went away silently to hunt supper for his hungry nestlings. A bat, with wings as quiet as Bubo's, flew above Walloon's lake, catching insects with his sharp teeth.

Telea did not hear Bubo call, and she knew nothing about Tha. But, like other night creatures, she became alert. She moved her wings and fluttered up to a near-by branch. She climbed the branch before she sailed away on a longer, swifter flight. Then she came to rest again, this time on the rough trunk of a tree.

As she clung there, Telea's body sent out a delicate odor. Neither Tha, Bubo, nor the bat could smell it—but 'Phemus, who was far away, could smell it very well. At once, he turned in his flight and started straight for Telea.

Who was 'Phemus? He was a large moth with "peacock-eye" markings on his wings. His feathery feelers were much wider than Telea's. They really were *smellers,* for 'Phemus used them to detect the odor that came from Telea's body. They told him just where to fly and where to stop. In three minutes, he alighted on the rough bark beside her.

Telea was no longer alone. She would have a comrade on her first evening in the woods.

CHAPTER XIV

PINI COLA, THE GROSBEAK WHO DWELT AMONG THE PINES

THERE are no hummingbirds flying about Europe or Asia or Africa. Like many other birds, they may be found only in North, South, and Central America. But you may meet pine grosbeaks if you go to the right places in Europe or Asia, as well as in America. In the summertime, the right places are northern forests where pines or other evergreens grow.

Pini Cola, the grosbeak of this story, however, does not live in Europe or Asia. He is spending this month of July in Canada. He has been there every summer of his life, arriving the last of May and staying until sometime in October. Perhaps it seems like going home, after a winter's journey; for Canada is the country in which Pini Cola first lived. That was when he had just hatched from one of the eggs his mother brooded in her nest.

Mother Grosbeak's feathers were mostly gray, though her head and rump were yellowish and she had two white barlike stripes across her wings. Father

Pini Cola perched on a lichen-covered hemlock branch.

Grosbeak's coat was rosy pink mixed with a little smoky gray, and his two wing bars were pinkish white. These colors were much like those of a male "purple finch," a bird whose head is really rosy red, whose back is reddish mixed with brownish gray, and whose upper breast is rose-pink rather than the color most people mean when they say *"purple."*

Pini Cola's own first winter suit was almost like those his mother and his sisters wore, except that the top of his head, parts of his back, and his rump had a slight reddish tinge. It was not until he was several years old, indeed, that his colors became as rich and rosy as those of his father.

When Pini Cola goes to Canada each spring, he does not travel alone. He has plenty of company, because he goes with a whole flock of pine grosbeaks. Their journey is not nearly so long as that of many birds. Pine grosbeaks do not need to fly to really warm places for their winter. Some of them go as far south as Kentucky or Kansas, but Pini Cola's companions stop in Maine. They fluff out their feathers and do not suffer during the cold winter days there. And the snow? Why, that is rather jolly. The grosbeaks like to play in it. At least, they act as if they were playing when they take a snow bath. They flutter their wings in the soft snow as if they were splashing in shallow water; and they keep their feathers clean and tidy. No, the snow and the cold do not trouble them, if they can find plenty to eat.

Did you ever see the snow under a highbush-cranberry shrub when it looked as if it had been dyed a pretty red? Grosbeaks like the seeds of these berries and drop the skin and most of the juicy, red pulp as they feed.

Pini Cola and his winter comrades have a great many feasts of highbush cranberries in Maine. So they color the snow red in different places. They eat the seeds of the red fruits of mountain ash and sumac, too. Seeds that fall from cones of firs and spruces, seeds that cling to maple and box elder and ash trees, are all on their bill of fare, as well as seeds of various other sorts. When they can find no seeds at all, they are satisfied to lunch on the winter leaf-buds of certain trees and shrubs.

These winter picnics are sociable affairs, and the grosbeaks speak pleasantly to one another as they fly from branch to branch. Pini Cola often perches on the top of a pine or spruce tree and calls to others of the flock, as if telling them where he is. He practices a song, too, and by spring he sings it well—a sweet, whistling warble that reminds one of the delightful music of a purple finch.

By early spring, Pini Cola and the other males of his flock are singing more and more. It is time then to fly northward. Some birds take rather straight flights, but the grosbeaks move up and down in a wavy way. And as they travel, they sing a flight song—and their voices go up and down, in a *teetering* sort of sound.

At this same time and over these same northward routes, flocks of other birds take their spring journeys. They, too, swing up and down in a wavy manner as they fly. They, too, have an up-and-down flight call. These

Birds Called "Purple" Finches

birds are the purple finches, which are described earlier in this chapter.

It is not strange that Pini Cola should look much like a purple finch, have much the same manner of flight, and sing a similar song; for Pini Cola belongs to the Finch Family. So he is a sort of cousin to the other finches.

What will Pini Cola be doing during late July and August and September, in Canada? His days will be carefree. The shallow nest on a low branch of an evergreen tree is already empty, for the sons and daughters that he and his mate fed insects for a while are now flying about. He, himself, will eat insects for part of his meals as well as blueberries and other summer fruits and seeds.

And what will those pine grosbeaks in Europe be doing these same summer days? Have you friends in northern Norway or Sweden? If so, why not write to them and ask what berries the pine grosbeaks are finding there to enjoy? Your friends will probably tell you that the pine grosbeaks they see like to eat the berries that grow on bushes belonging to the Heath Family—the very same family to which our blueberries belong.[9]

[9] In this connection, you may be interested to read "Heath Bells and Berries." a chapter in *Holiday Hill.*

CHAPTER XV

THE RUFFS

FATHER Ruff, the "drumming grouse" or partridge, spent most of the summer days in a carefree way. He wandered here and there in the forest, having a perfectly good time all by himself. Mother Ruff needed no help from her mate while she was brooding the eggs that filled her nest. She, herself, kept them warm for the twenty-four days before they hatched. Of course she did not sit on them every minute. She did not leave them in stormy weather, but on pleasant days she went away long enough to get all the food she wanted and to take some exercise. There were ten of the pale buff eggs in her nest this year. Some years there were more than ten, and one year she laid only seven.

Perhaps even Father Ruff did not know where his mate had hidden her nest. She was always very quiet when she crept through the thicket to the shallow hollow on the ground with a bed of brown, dry leaves under the eggs. There were a lot of brown, dry leaves on the ground near the nest, too. When Mother Ruff stepped out of her nest, she usually brushed some of these loose leaves over her eggs before she left them. Then they did not show.

Mother Ruff did not show, either, when she was on her nest. Once Ralph, son of the fire warden who spent the summer in a log cabin a mile away, wandered into the thicket. He did not notice the dappled, light and dark feathers on Mother Ruff's back as she sat in the midst of the streaky lights and shadows on the dry, brown leaves. He might have stepped on her if she had not done something that startled him so much that he jumped quickly and stumbled. Then he caught his foot against a young birch stem and fell over backwards.

How could the bird surprise a boy like that? When she saw him coming too near, she flew up suddenly, making a loud clapping and roaring racket with her wings. That is a performance that startles for a moment a forest guide who has heard it many times; and young Ralph had never seen and heard a partridge do that trick before.

Even after the eggs hatched, Father Ruff did not come to the nest and bring food to the ten hungry chicks. He just went off for rather long walks or short flights to places where he could find food for himself. He liked the tender buds of some herbs, vines, and bushes. Raspberries or blackberries or other small summer fruits always tasted good to him. When it was time for them to be ripe, he was glad to pick white snowberries and red bunchberries, checkerberries, and partridge berries. Now and then he ate an insect when he saw one he wanted. But he never thought of sharing the food he found.

Do not blame Father Ruff, however, for that was

126

Father Ruff took long walks through the woods.

the proper way for him to behave. Mother Ruff did not carry food to the nest, either. But you need not think that those ten little chicks starved. Not at all! They were not hungry, of course, when they first broke their way out of their eggshells and cuddled in the nest with their

Father Ruff ate berries like these: 1—partridge berry, or twinberry. 2—bunchberry. 3—spicy wintergreen or checkerberry. 4—snowberry, which is white. The other three berries are red.

feathers still damp. But soon their feathers were dry and fluffy; and their legs were so strong that they could toddle out of the nest before they had their first meal.

It was interesting to walk on the ground. Their mother spoke to them in her grouse language and they followed her. In a little while she picked up a very young caterpillar and dropped it in front of one of the chicks. The baby chick poked it with his tiny bill and then took hold of it and swallowed it. Soon he was finding little soft insects for himself. He ate spiders, too. He and his brothers and sisters liked insects and spiders better than buds or berries, while they were quite young. Such meat was good food for them.

Besides the roaring-flight trick Mother Grouse had played on Ralph that day in the thicket, she had another good trick. She played that on Ralph, too. One day she was leading her chicks through an opening, and Ralph met them there as he came down his favorite trail. He stopped to watch them. Mother Ruff said a quick grouse-word that meant "Hide, by keeping still!" Then she stumbled and flopped slowly along the trail in a crippled sort of way. Ralph thought she had a broken wing and was so sorry for her that he ran after her. He wanted to catch her and take her to his father to have her wing fixed.

But after Mother Ruff had led the boy far enough away from her chicks, she flew swiftly off into the forest. There was nothing the matter with her wing. She was only fooling Ralph—just as she would have fooled a fox, if she had wanted to lead one away from the young Ruffs.

There were only two grouse chicks in sight.

Father Ruff happened to be near enough to hear his mate when she called "Hide!" to her youngsters. He walked into the opening to see if his help was needed. There were only two chicks in sight. All the others were well hidden. Their father was standing still when Ralph came back along the trail.

That old grouse had not been so quiet the first time Ralph had seen him. One day in early spring, Ralph and his father were spending a week end together at the forest cabin. Toward dusk, Ruff came to a favorite place of his, which happened to be within sight of the cabin. He hopped to a fallen tree trunk and began to strut back and forth. His fan-shaped tail was spread like that of a strutting turkey cock. The crest on his head was raised. A ruff of feathers, on each side of his neck, was held spread out above a bare place underneath.

Then the ruffed grouse stopped strutting and began to move his wings. They went up above his back and down to his breast very swiftly—somehow making a loud *thump-thump-thump* that could be heard far through the forest. Old Ruff was "drumming"!

CHAPTER XVI

LITTLE VERSI, WHO CHANGED HIS COLORS

WHO was singing that tune in the woods, one cloudy day? The music had a pleasant, purring sort of trill. It sounded very near, though it really came from a place quite far away.

The singer was Hyla Versi-color, a full-grown frog about two inches long. He stopped his tune every time he took a leap. He was not hopping along the ground near the lake. He was jumping, like a circus acrobat, among the leafy branches of an old oak tree. You may know, from the way he was acting, that Versi was a tree frog.

Versi's full name fitted his habits. *Hyla* is a word meaning "woodland," or "forest." *Versi* means "change," and all of us know what *color* means. We may understand the whole name, then, to mean "woodland frog that changes color"—which is just what Versi was.

Often, while leaping from one branch to another, Versi would open his mouth and catch a fly or some other insect that was hovering near. He did not need to watch closely for his landing place, for he was in no danger of falling. Versi's fingers (four on each hand) and toes (five on each foot) all had disks that helped him cling to anything they touched—even if it was as smooth as glass.

Versi did not need to jump for his food unless he wished to get it that way. He could find small beetles and good-tasting caterpillars that were feeding on the oak leaves. Then, too, he liked to eat a lot of those tiny, juicy aphids which some people call "plant lice."

Perhaps, for weeks at a time, Versi would not go away from the big oak tree when he went hunting. There were plenty of insects right there for most of his meals. That suited him very well, for his summer home was an old deserted woodpecker's hole in the trunk of the oak; and he did not care to go far away. By hunting leaf-eating insects, he helped Bomby Cilla, Vireo, Veery, Pini Cola, and many other birds take care of the forest trees.

Trees have more leaves than they really need for their own use. They can spare some of them for Telea and other insects. But, of course, it is not good for them to lose too many leaves. That is why birds and tree frogs often help trees while they have a pleasant time hunting for their own food.

Versi's hole-home would have been his winter bedroom, too, if the wood there had been decayed. Then he could have dug with his hands to tuck himself into the soft, moist, crumbly wood. Versi would have liked a snug place right there in which to sleep during the

Versi hopped through these woods,
one evening in early spring.

cold weather. But the floor of that old woodpecker hole was not yet rotten enough for him to dig into. When autumn came, Versi left it and moved into a hollow under the matted brown leaves near the base of the tree for his winter bedroom. He usually went to sleep there in September and he did not waken until some warm day in the spring.

Versi did not invite anyone to share his summer home. He hunted alone and ate his meals alone. He lived by himself without needing companions—like a little hermit.

Of course, another tree frog sometimes leaped among the branches of Versi's oak or rested on the bark. But he and Versi gave no heed to each other. Neither even noticed what color the other one was wearing. Versi would be green if he sat on a green leaf for a while. So would the other tree frog. If either of them rested on a dark place of the trunk or branch, he would be wearing dark colors after an hour or so. If he spent some time on a mat of pale gray-green lichens, he would change his colors to match those of the lichens.

Versi and the other tree frog did not molt their skins when they changed their colors. In their skins, there were some layers of cells containing bits of coloring matter. Changes took place in these cells so that the skins of the tree frogs could nearly match the colors of things near their bodies.[10]

---

[10] More is told about the changing colors of tree frogs in "Safety First among Animals," a chapter in *The Work of Scientists.*

Versi became pale to match the colors of his lichen mat.
The other tree frog was dark because he rested on dark bark.

Versi, who lived without seeking friends during his tree days in the summer, did not have any roommates while he slept through the fall and winter months in his own little hollow under the brown leaves. But something happened to him after he wakened from his long winter's sleep. He did not feel, then, like climbing a tree and singing all by himself. We do not mean that Versi was silent during that pleasant spring season. He really sang a great deal, and so did all the other musical tree frogs in that part of the forest. But their songs were not solos, then. They had a chorus of male voices. At first it was not a big chorus. It started like a trio or quartet, with only three or four singers. That was because not all the tree frogs awoke the same day. Some of the winter bedrooms were in colder places than others, and the ice about them was longer in melting. So some of the sleepers were later in stretching their arms and legs, and they did not feel like getting up as soon as their warmer neighbors.

But each evening, and on every cloudy day, more and more trills could be heard. And each evening the voices sounded closer together, for all the singers were going to the same place. They were hopping to the edge of a little lake and trilling loudly on their way.

At last, at the shallow margin of the lake, the chorus music was most joyous. Not even a spring flock of blackbirds coming to their northern homes to nest, after their winter in the South, gives a happier concert than did those trilling tree frogs.

You have watched birds sing and have noticed that

they open their mouths, as people open theirs—unless they are merely humming. Did Versi also hold his big mouth open while he sang? No, he kept it shut.

Each male tree frog can puff out the loose membrane under his chin into a *throat sac,* or *chin sac,* as it is sometimes called. This sac is empty when the frog is not singing, and it does not show then. But when the frog sings, his throat sac is full of air. How does the air get into the sac? First the tree frog breathes the air through his nostrils into his lungs. Next he forces air from his lungs into his closed mouth. Then he forces this air from his mouth, through openings near the base of his tongue, into his throat sac. Thus the throat

When tree frogs sing, their throat sacs puff out like little balloons.

sac puffs out like a tiny toy balloon. The air rushing in and out of the sac makes the voice of the singer much louder than it could be without this music pouch.

There is no doubt that Versi and his comrades had a good time trilling and humming in this way. Otherwise they would have stopped. But they were not the only ones who were pleased with that music.

Many silent tree frogs liked the tune so well that they simply could not stay away. So they came hopping to the lake to listen to the concert, and meet the singers.

The listeners looked very much like the singers, though their throats were not so dark and they had no chin sacs. The concert singers and the listeners played in the water together. They would rather swim than climb trees this time of year. They paddled about with their partly webbed hands and feet.

One of the listeners became Versi's mate. She laid a lot of pale yellowish-gray eggs in a mass near the surface of the water among the stems of water plants. The eggs were covered with some soft, colorless stuff that looked like clear gelatin.

After about four days, baby tadpoles hatched from these eggs. At first the tadpoles were almost a quarter of an inch long, with big heads, no legs, and long flat tails. They became very pretty—their shiny bodies had golden tints, their tails were scarlet and edged with black spots and their eyes were bright and gleaming. Each tadpole grew to be two inches long from the tip of his head to the tip of his long tail. Changes took place in the shape of the body. The tail became shorter and shorter while the rest of the body grew broader; two hind legs grew out and later two front legs were pushed through the skin.

When the Versi children were seven or eight weeks old, they were not tadpoles any more. They were tailless little tree frogs only little more than half an inch long. You see, their bodies became shorter as they lost their long tails.

By this time, the young tree frogs were ready to stop swimming and to begin to climb. They started early in the morning before the sun was up. The first things they found to climb were sedges growing in the lake. So they crept up the sedge stems and out on the long, narrow leaves that drooped over the water. They sat in little rows on the sedge leaves for a while. Their green color just matched that of the leaves on which they perched.

By evening, the frogs had hopped to some arrowhead plants nearer the edge of the lake. There they found some plump little aphids which they ate for their first supper above water. While under water, their food had been soft bits they nibbled from tender plants and soft decaying things they found.

A few evenings later, Versi's sons and daughters were leaping here and there on some bushes a little way from the lake. There they found aphids of a different kind—but just as good to eat as those on the arrowheads.

Though these little tree frogs were brothers and sisters, they did not stay together in a family group. Each one climbed and hopped off by himself or herself.

Each was satisfied to be hunting alone, or finding his own nice, damp, shady place where the sun was not too hot. None of them missed his brothers and sisters—or his father and mother either.

The old tree frogs had left the lake while their children were still tadpoles. Versi was now back in his favorite oak tree, singing a solo every evening and on cloudy days. Versi, Junior, one of his sons, happened to hop on a leaf near Versi one day; but the youngster did not even know what a father tree frog looked like.

Perhaps this is not so strange as it seems, since Versi so often changed his colors. Junior's father might be green when his son saw him one day; and he might be gray or brown the next time.

And whether green or gray or brown, whether singing in a spring concert at the lake or trilling summer solos in his tree, Versi seemed to be having a pleasant time! [11]

[11] Other accounts of tree frogs like Hyla Versi-color are: "The Common Tree Frog" in *The Frog Book*, and "The Cabin of the Common Tree Frog" in *First Lessons in Nature Study*.

CHAPTER XVII

THE BEAVERS OF POPLAR CREEK

THE moon was shining as Amisk, the beaver, swam up Poplar Creek. He had been traveling since dusk, just as he had done almost every night during July and early August. He had swum in rivers and across lakes. He had hurried through ponds where other beavers had built their dome-shaped houses. He had paddled up streams shaded by willows and alders. He liked the taste of alder bark, and often ate a meal of it when he stopped to rest.

As Amisk traveled, he looked for a place to build his own home. He should choose a house lot before September began, for autumn was the time for building. But, till he reached Poplar Creek, not one place pleased him. Rivers were too swift, lakes were too large, and ponds either belonged to other beavers or had few good food trees on their shores.

Poplar Creek, however, seemed just what Amisk wanted. Pines, spruces, and hemlocks grew on the hills near it, but groves of poplars stood on its banks. There also were paper birches, speckled alders, and willows of

*Amisk swam across ponds where other beavers
had built dome-shaped homes.*

several kinds. Each had bark which beavers considered very good food.

Yes, Poplar Creek was just right for a home. But Amisk did not wish to build a house all by himself and live in it alone. He wanted a mate who would live there with him, and help him enjoy Poplar Creek.

Was there another beaver near by? Amisk did not see one, nor hear one, but he had another way of finding out. As he swam up the creek, he watched for banks of mud or clay. At each bank, he dug a lump and patted it into a little mud cake. Then he laid the cake on the ground at the water's edge and put some beaver musk on it. The musk, which had a strong odor, came from two glands in his body. It turned each mud cake into a message. The message meant, "A lonely beaver has come to this creek. He wants to meet another beaver."

When his last mud cake was made, Amisk ate an alder-bark breakfast and went to sleep under some roots. The next evening, he swam to the first mud cake and sniffed it. It was not touched, nor was any of the others. Not even a muskrat had smelled them with his damp, black nose.

Amisk was not discouraged. He came the next night, and the next, putting a few new cakes here and there. On the following evening, he began with the most distant cake.

It was just as he had left it, so he paddled on. A weasel had sniffed the cake nearest it; and a porcupine had walked across another, scraping it with his spines. Then Amisk came to a cake that had a fresh smell of

Groves of poplars, or aspens, grew near Poplar Creek.

musk, and showed prints of a beaver's nose and paw. Notsa, another beaver, had been there and had left her scented message for Amisk.

Amisk found Notsa near some willows, not very far away. She was glad to see him; for she, too, had felt a bit lonely. She greeted him with a whispering sound, and Amisk answered with a soft murmur. Then the two beavers rubbed noses and ate a meal of willow bark. They were so happy that they decided to be mates and live on Poplar Creek together.

For a few nights, they swam up and down the creek; in daytime, they slept under overhanging roots. For their breakfasts (which came when they wakened after sunset), they cut willows, alders, and poplars with their teeth, which were almost as sharp as chisels. Then they peeled off the coarse outer bark and ate the light-colored, sweetish bark that was near the wood.

As they swam, the beavers looked for a place in which to build a dam. At last they found one—where the creek was shallow, and its valley was wide. And near it were plenty of trees whose bark was best for food.

Then Amisk and Notsa set to work. Each cut a branch of alder and swam to a low ridge of gravel, where Poplar Creek was shallowest. Such a bank made a good foundation for a beaver dam.

Notsa reached the gravel bank first. She pushed the cut end of her alder branch into it, with the twigs pointing upstream. For a moment, it almost floated away. Then the current pushed it into the gravel. When

Leaves and wood of some trees whose bark Amisk ate: 1—poplar (Quaking Aspen). 2—balsam poplar. 3—black willow. 4—peach-leaved willow. 5—a cut stick of paper birch, partly peeled. Notice the marks of Amisk's teeth.

it seemed safe, Amisk placed his branch beside Notsa's and both beavers swam away.

All night long, the beavers brought sticks and newly cut branches. They placed the first ones near the bank, the next ones farther out, and the next ones still farther. If the branches started to move, the beavers piled stones on them. When morning came, they had a low wall across nearly one-third of the creek. They took three more nights to work their way across it. They stopped long enough to nibble bark when they were hungry; and, of course, they slept during the day.

After the first row of branches was placed, the beavers cut larger pieces of alder and poplar. They tugged these to the water and piled them among the small ones—making a good framework of the dam. They also brought stones, which helped hold the sticks in place. Finally, the two beavers packed grassy mud against the upstream side of the dam, until almost every crack was filled.

When the dam was finished, it held back enough water to make a pleasant pond. It also turned a grassy knoll into a little island. Amisk and Notsa chose this island as a foundation for their house. First, they dug a long tunnel which slanted upward to the surface. Next they put mud, roots, and sticks on the island, around the tunnel door, and made a heap of old branches and other rubbish about two feet high at one side of the door.

They laid long alder sticks against this high part, covering them with more rubbish. They kept on building with mud, sticks, and branches until they had

Amisk and Notsa built their house of sticks and mud.

a dome-shaped mound four feet high and ten feet wide. This they covered with muddy grass and small sticks and plastered it over with a thick outer layer of mud. They left an open tangle of sticks at the top, however. This would let fresh air in, when the beavers made their living room.

The living room was cut, not built. First Notsa slipped into the tunnel and climbed to the long alder sticks. She began to gnaw parts of them away, and to pull out chunks of mud. When she was tired, Amisk took her place. Both beavers carried the waste mud and sticks to the dam. In time, they had cleared out a room in their big mound. It was dark, snug, and safe. One part of its floor was higher than the rest of it. The beavers covered the higher part with grass and shreds of bark, turning it into a comfortable bed.

It was a nuisance to have only one tunnel, when the beavers tried to hurry. Notsa ran into Amisk twice. Then she dug a new tunnel. It was short and very steep. Notsa could dive through it while Amisk was going halfway down the first one. She could leave the house for a game of water tag and be ready to duck her mate the moment he came from the door!

Even when the dam and the house were finished, Amisk and his mate cut more and more trees. They gnawed at the trunk of each tree until it was ready to fall. Then they hurried to one side so it could not hit them when it crashed to the ground. But soon they came back to trim off its limbs and to gnaw the trunk

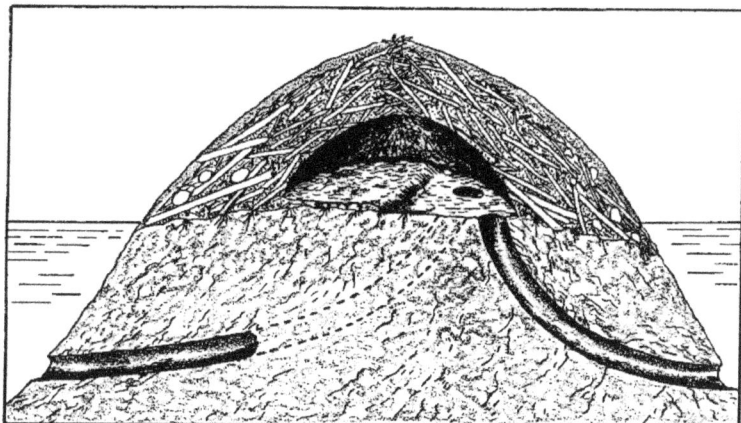

Section of the house built by Amisk and Notsa—
showing living room and the two tunnel-hallways.

into sections short enough for them to drag. They often spent two nights cutting up a single tree.

The beavers did not use this wood for building. They swam with it across the pond, till they reached a spot near their house. Then they dived to the bottom, fastening some of the sticks to roots and poking others into the mud. After a time, they had three big piles anchored so firmly that they could not float away.

Of course, Amisk and Notsa had not done all this work in the one month of September. They were busy every night in October and toiled, too, during early November. By this time, ice had begun to form at the edge of their pond.

Then, one cold November day, winds brought a storm howling down from the North. The storm bent and tossed the tops of the leafless trees, whirled across the pond, and left snowdrifts on the banks.

Even after that first snow, Amisk went back to work as soon as evening came. He helped Notsa cut up the last of a poplar and drag it down to the pond. Then he found a good tree of his own. Sitting on the very top of a snowdrift, he began to bite into it.

Morning came before the tree fell, and Amisk had to leave it standing. That day the sun shone warmly, melting the snowdrift. When Amisk came back to the tree at sunset, he found last night's cut too high for him to reach with his teeth. He had to start cutting all over again at a lower place on the trunk. It had been a waste of time to perch on a drift of snow while he worked the night before.

Amisk and Notsa worked very hard all the next night, too. They cut a lot of branches and tucked them into the wood piles. By morning, the winds were howling down from the North again, bringing another storm. This time it left snowdrifts that did not melt and a coat of ice on the pond that grew thicker every day.

What did it matter? The two beavers had had a good time working all the fall; but now they could be just as happy staying inside their house night and day. It was time for them to enjoy their home. Its thick walls kept out the wind. The warmth of their own bodies took the chill from the room, while the hole left at its very top let fresh air in and allowed the stale air to go out.

Didn't they get too hungry? No, indeed! When Notsa wanted some bark to eat, she dived into one of the passageways that opened in her floor. Coming out of the house, she swam under the ice to the wood pile, which was really a food pile. She tugged at a stick till it came loose and swam back to the house. Her fur was dripping but she let the water drain on the floor. Then she peeled the coarse outer bark from the soaked stick and ate the good-tasting whitish inner bark. Later she would carry the peeled stick down the passageway and drop it into the water where it could drift to the dam. Such peeled food-sticks would be handy for repairs on the dam during the next summer.

Amisk, too, brought in a supply of food every now and then. The winter meals which the two beavers ate together seemed as good to them as that breakfast of willow bark they had enjoyed the first morning they met beside Poplar Creek.

CHAPTER XVIII

BOMBY AND VIREO

Bomby Cilla, Who Whispered

Does Bomby Cilla seem a strange name for a bird? *Bomby* is an old word meaning "silk," and *cilla* is sometimes used instead of "tail." So you may call Bomby Cilla "Silktail" if you like that name any better. Or you may call him "Waxwing," for that is one of his names, too.

You may guess that he had glossy feathers, or people would not have thought about such shiny things as silk and wax when they were naming him.

Perhaps you may remember something about another bird so glossy that he was given a name that meant "shining-robe-shining," with "Pep" for a nickname.[12] Bomby Cilla, by the way, was a rather close relative of Pep, so it is not strange that they both wore suits of very shiny feathers. Bomby had a crest on his head, too, shaped much like Pep's crest, and this added to his elegant looks.

The two handsome relatives did not wear the

[12] "Pep, Who Wore a Shining Robe," in *Desert Neighbors*.

same colors, though. Pep, as you may remember, was gleaming black with a white patch on each wing. The feathers on most of Bomby's body were grayish-brown with a pink or purplish tinge. On the underside, he was yellow in front of his legs and white near his tail. His tail was blackish-gray with a straight, yellow tip. Some of his gray wing feathers were tipped with red of about the shade of bright red sealing wax. His face looked as if he were wearing a mask, for he had a velvety black band across his forehead above his bill, and his chin was black.

If you had seen Bomby one bright, sunny, September afternoon, you might have thought that he seemed to be all dressed up to go to some fancy party—with his crest for a crown, his black mask, and the gay yellow and red trimmings on his satiny suit.

Well, Bomby really did go to a party that afternoon, and he had a very good time. It was a pleasant party in a chokecherry thicket at the edge of the woods.

In the spring, soon after the fresh, new leaves had grown, the small trees in this thicket had been beautiful. Then slender, green spikes, crowded with little white flowers, were dangling from their branches. Some of the spikes were more than five inches long, so there was room on them for many blossoms. These same spikes still hung from the branches that day in September, but there were no flowers on them then. In place of the blossoms, there were little, dark crimson cherries, each with one smooth, stony seed inside.

If you have ever eaten wild cherries of this sort

(before they are fully ripe or frosted), you know that the juicy pulp gives you a puckery, choky feeling in your throat. That is why they are called "chokecherries." But they did not choke Bomby. It was because he liked the taste of them that he came to the thicket for a feast.

Some other Waxwings were at the thicket party, too; but Bomby did not chatter merrily with them. He gave a little lisping sort of squeaking whisper when he first arrived. His comrades whispered now and then as they moved about but they were silent much of the time. They all had very quiet manners.

As soon as Bomby picked every cherry from one drooping spike, he flitted to another perch where he could get more cherries. He kept eating until he could not swallow another mouthful. A spike full of ripe cherries almost touched his bill, but he did not reach up to it. He sat still, too lazy to move.

After a time, five of the other Waxwings settled on the branch beside Bomby. Their coming seemed to rouse Bomby a bit. He stretched his head up a little and picked a cherry. It was a very good cherry but he had no room for it. Whatever should he do? In another moment he turned his head and tucked the cherry into the half-open beak of the bird next to him. The second bird did not want it either but he did not drop it. Perhaps it seemed too good to be wasted. He followed Bomby's example and placed it in the mouth of the third bird. In this manner the cherry went down to the sixth bird at the end of the line.

This last bird in the row started to hand the cherry

*Bomby and other Waxwings had their party
in the chokecherry thicket.*

back to the friend who had given it to him. Then he paused with his mouth open. The cherry dropped to the ground. Well, it didn't really matter. It might be rather fun to play this cherry-passing game; but maybe it was silly, after all, to keep at it when the birds had already eaten so much that they felt lazy.

Chokecherry banquets were not the only feasts Bomby enjoyed. During the summer and fall, he ate wild berries of almost any kind he could find near his home.

He did not depend altogether on a fruit diet, however. He liked insect meat, too—especially the tender little caterpillars called "inchworms." During two or three weeks he ate about a thousand of these, so you see he really did like them. Besides, he fed a thousand or two more to his young ones. It was fortunate that he did so, too; for these inchworms were very thick that year. So thick, indeed, that many of the trees would have lost all their leaves, if Waxwings and other birds had not come to their rescue.

We have spoken of Bomby's quiet whispers during the September chokecherry party. He had been quiet all summer, too. Now and then he gave a wheezy whisper that you could not have heard unless you had been within a few feet of him. In the spring, to be sure, he had warbled a few soft, low tunes. That was about the time he met the Waxwing who became Mrs. Bomby Cilla.

Indeed, the only time in his life when Bomby had voiced a really loud call was one day of the last week in June. It was about six o'clock in the morning and Bomby was hunting for some good fibers to use in building his nest. The best ones he found happened to be pieces of string tied to a branch. A forest ranger, who liked birds, had fastened a chunk of suet on a branch sometime during the winter months. Chickadees, nuthatches, and woodpeckers had eaten every bit of the suet but they had left the string.

Well, Bomby wanted that string! He tugged at it as hard as he could but it did not come off the branch. After a while he became very much annoyed and at last he was so distressed that he yelled for help. His voice sounded very loud indeed—at least, for a Waxwing's. A whisper was not enough for him just then!

Mrs. Cilla heard the screech and hurried to her mate. She saw what he was trying to do, and sat on the branch near him and did her part in giving the string violent jerks.

Working together, these birds managed to tear a few shreds from the string. They were glad to use them in their nest, along with other fibers.

It really was too bad that the forest ranger didn't come along just then. If he had seen those Waxwings struggling to get the string, he would have taken out his knife and cut it into short lengths for them. But he was miles away that June morning and so couldn't hear Bomby screaming for help.

And so it happened that the forest ranger, like many other people, never learned that the Waxwing *can*, if he is excited enough, speak louder than in a thin, wheezy whisper.

OLIVER VIREO, WHO "PREACHED"

Many of Bomby's bird neighbors had good spring songs, loud and strong enough to be heard by visitors in the forest. But during the hot summer days, even they were quiet. At least, most of them were. Oliver, the red-eyed Vireo, was an exception. He kept on singing all summer. He did not stop even during the heat of a sunny noon.

Oliver would sing several notes, with his voice going up as if asking a question. Then he would pause for a moment before singing what seemed like another short question. It was as if he were giving the listener time to think about what he was asking.

A man named Wilson Flagg once listened to a red-eyed Vireo, and then he called him a "preacher." That was nearly sixty years ago; but people have thought Wilson Flagg's name such a good one that they have called these Vireos "preachers" ever since.

What was Oliver preaching about? Of course he was not really preaching at all; but each person who hears him may imagine words to suit himself.

Perhaps, if you hear one of these birds someday and notice what he is *doing,* you may put his questions this way:

> "Here, here—see this little plump one?
> See me catch a caterpillar? There's one now!
> Need you really dust or spray this tree bough?
> Think you really need to—when I've done?
> Let me hunt the caterpillars? Lots of fun!"

Oliver sat in an alder shrub and "preached"
while his mate was busy.

You may not be sure what words to put to his humdrum little tune. But if you watch his actions, you can have no doubt at all about his help in taking care of trees. And certainly he has a happy time from dawn until evening.

Many songsters stop most of their music during nest-building time while they are helping their mates. But Oliver's tune could be heard late in May while Olive was busy with her nest. Perhaps Oliver did not help as much as some father birds do; but he followed his mate back and forth when she was gathering fibers for building. At least he seemed interested.

Olive's nest was worth being interested in. It hung down from the fork of a branch of a young poplar tree. It was not so deep as an oriole's hanging nest but was shaped more like a cup. Olive bound the edges firmly over the branch with tough strips of inner bark from the stem of a young broken tree. She used some of the stout outer fibers of old goldenrod stems, too. But she was not satisfied to have merely a strong nest with a soft-padded lining. She decorated the outside with bits of light-colored things. She tore off some paper from an empty hornets' nest. She picked up scraps of a newspaper a forest ranger had left near a camp site. She tucked in bits of silken web torn from a tent caterpillar's "tent," and finished up with little white silken cocoons which spiders had spun to hold their eggs.

When the dappled gray and white nest was finished, it hardly showed in the light and shade among the pale branches of the tree. You might have passed very near it without seeing it.

That is, you might not have noticed it if the quiet Olive was sitting on her eggs. But if it were Oliver's turn, you might have heard his voice and looked to see where he was. For, strange to say, he did not stop his chatty little tune even while he was on the nest.

So you see that "preaching" Oliver did not behave at all like his neighbor, "whispering" Bomby. Olive and Oliver Vireo did not look like Mr. and Mrs. Bomby Cilla, either. They had olive-green backs and the tops of their smooth heads were gray. Each eye looked like a pretty red jewel with a white streak above it and a narrow black line between the white and the gray head-top.

We think you would like both the Waxwings and the Vireos. It would be worth a trip to some northern forest just to meet them.

But, as perhaps you know, you would not need to go a great many miles to see these birds. For Waxwings build their nests where there are trees, in most of North America. And the cup-shaped nests of red-eyed Vireos may be found as far south as Florida.

A BOOK LIST

In connection with certain subjects in *Forest Neighbors*, references have been made to chapters or articles in the following books:

Bird Stories, by Edith M. Patch.

Desert Neighbors, by Edith M. Patch and Carroll Lane Fenton.

First Lessons in Nature Study, by Edith M. Patch.

The Frog Book, by Mary C. Dickerson.

Holiday Hill, by Edith M. Patch.

Mountain Neighbors, by Edith M. Patch and Carroll Lane Fenton.

Science at Home, by Edith M. Patch. and Harrison E. Howe.

Surprises, by Edith M. Patch.

Through Four Seasons, by Edith M. Patch and Harrison E. Howe.

The Work of Scientists, by Edith M. Patch and Harrison E. Howe.

www.ingramcontent.com/pod-product-compliance
Lightning Source LLC
Chambersburg PA
CBHW031845090426
42741CB00005B/361